The Gothic Revival Style in America, 1830–1870

The Gothic Revival Style in America, 1830–1870

By Katherine S. Howe
and David B. Warren

With an introduction by Jane B. Davies

An Exhibition of Decorative Arts

April 1 through June 6, 1976

The Museum of Fine Arts, Houston

All photographs were supplied by the lenders or by Helga Photo Studios, Inc., except the following: Helga Photo Studios, Inc., for the magazine *Antiques*, 90; Jeannie Barnum, 107; E. Irving Blomstrann, 6; Edward Bourdon, 144; Will Brown, 8, 9, 52, 59, 93, 99, 155, 183; J. Byler, 33; Lin Caufield Photographers, Inc., 175; Richard Cheek, 20, 21, 22, 53, 56, 57, 58, 85, 95, 106, 148, 152, 186; George M. Cushing, 179; Manuel C. Delerno, 87; Thomas Anthony Donovan, 46; William Howze, 98, 101, 143a; Karas, 105; Le Boeuf Studios, 48, 107; Richard Merrill, 37, 151; Allen Mewbourn, 31, 47, 70a, 71a, 87a, 117, 138, 139, 194; Jinny and Wendy Neephus, 145, 145a; Pearlman-McNee Productions, 51, 81, 91; Rowles Studio, 88; Schopplein Studio, 115; Sleepy Hollow Studio, 12, 13, 14, 15, 17, 70, 71, 72, 96; Joseph Szaszfai, 92, 143; Herbert Vose, 171. The St. Louis Art Museum and the New York State Historical Association provided photographs for private lenders 133 and 154 respectively.

This exhibit is supported by a grant from the National Endowment for the Arts in Washington, D.C., a Federal agency.

Copyright © by The Museum of Fine Arts, Houston
Library of Congress Catalogue Number 76-9009
Published by The Museum of Fine Arts, Houston
Printed in the United States of America

Preface

On the eve of our nation's two-hundredth birthday, America has already experienced many celebrations focusing on her achievements both old and new. To them is now added "The Gothic Revival Style in America, 1830–1870," an exhibition organized to explore one of the major historical revival styles of the nineteenth century.

Why, the question might be asked, has this institution chosen to examine a style from the nineteenth century rather than to explore the taste of our colonial forefathers? The Museum of Fine Arts, Houston, is fortunate to have at Bayou Bend a remarkable collection spanning two centuries of American arts. That collection was brought together by the late Miss Ima Hogg to make available to the people of Texas and the Southwest the heritage of their colonial ancestors and was generously donated by her to the Museum. It stands as a permanent celebration of America's past, not only in the era before the Revolution, but also in the republican years and the early nineteenth century. A temporary loan exhibition examining the colonial taste would duplicate what is already available here.

In addition, modern American culture is far more a product of the nineteenth century in terms of attitudes, tastes, institutions, social systems, and customs than it is a product of the eighteenth century. Because Texas was born in the nineteenth century, it seemed particularly appropriate for this museum to consider a style from that era. The Gothic Revival is a taste that heretofore has received little or no formal attention. This exhibition is the first attempt to take an overview of that style.

WILLIAM C. AGEE
Director

Acknowledgments

In 1971 when the idea for this exhibition was first conceived, Philippe de Montebello, then director of the Museum of Fine Arts, Houston, gave his enthusiastic support to the project and encouraged us to begin immediately. Dean Frederick Failey, associate curator of the Bayou Bend Collection (1971–1974), did much of the preliminary work and made many initial contacts both with collectors and with other museums. His effort was an invaluable step in the long evolution from idea to reality.

The exhibition derives its importance from its concentration on a major nineteenth-century revival style that never before has received individual consideration. One of the joys of "discovering" a decorative style such as the Gothic Revival is the interesting route the discovery takes and the generous people who mark the way. Our search took us to Maryland warehouses, Michigan storage closets, East Texas living rooms, and into the homes, galleries, and offices of enthusiastic collectors, dealers, and curators. Each contributor has suffered the endless telephone calls and tedious letters necessary for planning a long-distance exhibition, and to a person each has responded with cheerful help.

A few lenders deserve special thanks: Lee B. Anderson, who probably knows more about America's Gothic Revival than anyone else, has generously shared both his knowledge and his collection with us; Anne C. Golovin at the Smithsonian Institution has counseled us on the Harral-Wheeler House, while Susan N. Lehman, formerly at the Smithsonian, shared with us several new discoveries; Letitia Galbraith, William C. Taggatt, and Pearson Marvin at the National Trust for Historic Preservation and Richard C. Nylander at the Society for the Preservation of New England Antiquities have answered many questions and have gracefully faced barren exhibition rooms as Lyndhurst and Roseland begin their busy seasons; David A. Hanks at the Philadelphia Museum of Art frequently worked on our behalf as did Robert G. Wheeler at Greenfield Village and the Henry Ford Museum; and lastly, our sincere thanks to Adolf K. Placzek and Eleanor N. Thompson at Avery Architectural Library, who graciously assisted our researchers and who made the extraordinary gesture of lending us six Alexander Jackson Davis drawings.

Many people directly involved in producing this catalogue deserve special recognition: Judith Winslow Blood and Joan Barenholtz ably did research for us in the New York area; Dianne R.

Binford was the accurate and uncomplaining worker who has typed everything pertinent to the exhibition; Barry A. Greenlaw, curator of the Bayou Bend Collection, reviewed the catalogue; Kate S. Leader was our fine and efficient editor; Edward B. Mayo, the museum's registrar, and his staff coordinated the arrival of the exhibition; E. M. Stone and his department together with Robert Spangler and his staff made the installation possible. Finally, Jane B. Davies not only wrote our introduction but also very graciously shared with us both her time and years of research on Alexander Jackson Davis. To each of these individuals and to our supportive families, our sincere thanks.

The National Endowment for the Arts deserves special recognition for a generous grant that partially funded this exhibition.

Until recently the Gothic Revival style in the United States has been an amusing but largely neglected phase in American decorative arts. The style has been the subject of very little research, and this catalogue offers a first retrospective view. The material shown here varies greatly and includes fine paintings and furniture as well as humble utilitarian objects. Some items are well documented while very little is known about others. The preponderance of chairs, probably the most commonly made form, and the frequent reference to Andrew Jackson Downing and Alexander Jackson Davis, the most prolific proponents of the style, have resulted in what may seem a disproportionate emphasis that has by no means been our intention. Years of grime on furniture not yet cherished has made it difficult to identify many of the woods used, and most were not microscopically tested. (Those from Stephen R. Parks, the Harral-Wheeler House, hall chair no. 47, and selected pieces from Roseland are exceptions.) This catalogue should not be construed as a definitive work; rather, it is a pioneering look at a delightful, romantic phase of American decorative arts that deserves to be explored in greater detail. It is hoped this exhibition will encourage that exploration.

October 30, 1975

KATHERINE S. HOWE
DAVID B. WARREN

Lenders to the Exhibition

Albany Institute of History and Art, Albany, New York
Lee B. Anderson
Avery Architectural Library, Columbia University, New York, New York
The Estate of Mrs. Hubert F. Barnum, Natchez, Mississippi
The Bayou Bend Collection, The Museum of Fine Arts, Houston, Texas
Mr. and Mrs. James Biddle
Joan and Bruce Bogart
The Brooklyn Museum, Brooklyn, New York
Frank Brozyna
Jay E. Cantor
Child's Gallery, Boston, Massachusetts
Colorado Springs Fine Arts Center, Colorado Springs, Colorado
Cooper-Hewitt Museum of Design, Smithsonian Institution, New York, New York
The Corning Museum of Glass, Corning, New York
The Detroit Institute of Arts, Detroit, Michigan
Essex Institute, Salem, Massachusetts
The Fine Arts Museums of San Francisco, San Francisco, California
Greenfield Village and the Henry Ford Museum, Dearborn, Michigan
David Allen Hanks, Philadelphia, Pennsylvania
Mrs. Stanley Hanks
The Harris County Heritage Society, Houston, Texas
Peter Hill, United States Antiques, Washington, D.C.
William J. Jedlick
C. R. and Susan C. Jones, Cooperstown, New York
The Keyes Foundation, New Orleans, Louisiana
Mrs. Charles H. Lewis
Henry H. Livingston
Louisiana State Museum, New Orleans, Louisiana
Lyman Allyn Museum, New London, Connecticut
Lyndhurst, National Trust for Historic Preservation, Tarrytown, New York
Maryland Historical Society, Baltimore, Maryland
The Metropolitan Museum of Art, New York, New York
Munson-Williams-Proctor Institute, Utica, New York
Museum of Fine Arts, Boston, Massachusetts
Museum of the City of New York, New York
The National Archives, Washington, D.C.
National Gallery of Art, Washington, D.C.
The National Museum of History and Technology, Smithsonian Institution, Washington, D.C.
National Park Service, Longfellow National Historic Site, Cambridge, Massachusetts
New Haven Colony Historical Society, New Haven, Connecticut
New York State Historical Association, Cooperstown, New York
The Newark Museum, Newark, New Jersey
Stephen Parks, New Haven, Connecticut
Philadelphia Museum of Art, Philadelphia, Pennsylvania
Hester Halstead Pier
Private Collections
The St. Louis Art Museum, St. Louis, Missouri
Anne and David Sellin
Sleepy Hollow Restorations, Tarrytown, New York
Smithsonian Institution, Washington, D.C.
Society for the Preservation of New England Antiquities, Boston, Massachusetts
The Stowe-Day Foundation, Hartford, Connecticut
Charles V. Swain
The Western Reserve Historical Society, Cleveland, Ohio
Graham Williford, Fairfield, Texas

Introduction

"The Gothic or English cottage . . . [is] just now the ambition of almost every person building in the country," wrote Andrew Jackson Downing in July 1850[1] at the height of the Gothic Revival style as a fashion in America for country houses and the decorative arts. Charming cottages with high gables and intricately carved vergeboards and enchanting villas with towers, turrets, pinnacles, and battlements appeared across the country, suggesting the mystery and fantasy of remote medieval times, while pointed arches, quatrefoils, trefoils, and crockets graced a myriad of household objects to recall the days of "Knighthood's dauntless deed and Beauty's matchless eye."[2]

In America the three decades before the Civil War were a period of restless exuberance and aspiration. This was a period also when an awakened sensitivity to the wonders of the American landscape exerted a forceful influence on the arts, giving rise to the Hudson River School of landscape painters and to such writers as William Cullen Bryant, James Fenimore Cooper, and Nathaniel P. Willis. This sensitivity to nature found its architectural expression in the emergence of American Picturesque styles for country houses—Romantic architecture for Romantic landscapes.

The Gothic Revival[3] was foremost among these styles—Italianate, Swiss, and Bracketed were others—and it was the most revolutionary of the period's many revival modes, which included also Greek, Egyptian, Renaissance, Elizabethan, and, in furniture, Rococo. Turning away from the classicism that had dominated architecture since the Renaissance, the Gothic Revival style looked to the Middle Ages for inspiration and reintroduced a vocabulary of forms and motifs that had been dormant and disdained for centuries, interpreting them anew for use in modern buildings and the decorative arts. The style in America had many aspects and developed in several stages. Its origins reached far back to the seventeenth century in England and on the Continent, and its manifestations extended on through the first half of the twentieth century. It was widely used for many types of buildings, especially for churches and colleges, but the chief concern here is with the Gothic Revival as a style for houses and their furnishings in the middle half of the nineteenth century, when it was the most romantic of the styles that flourished in America.

The Gothic Revival expressed the very quintessence of Romanticism—bold, dramatic, closely linked to nature, a visual evocation of the brooding melancholy and mystery of the remote Middle Ages so cherished by the Romantic spirit. It offered exuberant release from the restraints of classical tradition. Instead of prescribed orders, proportions, and symmetry, instead of time-worn motifs and the severity, rigidity, and limitations of the Greek Revival, it gave exhilarating and boundless freedom for creative activity. The intention was not to copy specific medieval buildings and objects with archeological exactness. Rather, through adaptation of typical motifs, it was to suggest impressions and arouse associations in the mind and heart that would recall the idealized vision of the Middle Ages as depicted in poetry, legend, and romantic novels.

Although America has a medieval heritage from its early days, the inspiration for its Gothic Revival came not from its own heritage but from the Gothic Revival abroad, chiefly as it developed in England. Americans returning from travels and sojourns in England, foreign-trained architects, and illustrated books of building views, designs, and details brought the style across the Atlantic. The American versions were free interpretations, distinct from their foreign sources of inspiration. They were adapted to the needs, the scale, and the materials of American building, for as Alexander Jackson Davis once wrote about English country-house designs, "the English plans are [either] on a scale far more extended and expensive than we can accomplish with our limited means; or . . . they are too inconsiderable and humble for the proper pride of republicans."[4]

In England, Classical supplanted Gothic as the prevalent style by the mid-seventeenth century, and real knowledge of the Gothic mode was mostly lost. It was only gradually regained as the renewed use of the style developed through a number of stages. The first two, the "Rococo" and especially the "Picturesque," are of greatest interest. They largely form the background for the American Gothic Revival of the Romantic period, before the Gothic Revival became seriously archeological, "honestly" structural, and fervently religious in its Early and High Victorian phases.

The reawakening of interest in the Middle Ages was influenced by antiquarian research and the writings of literary men. The poetic veneration of melancholy ruins, the study and imitation of early ballads, and later the gothic novels and the works of Sir Walter Scott, all gave a strong literary flavor to the early revival. In the late seventeenth and early eighteenth centuries Sir Christopher Wren and his followers on occasion used an approximation of Gothic, and Sir John Vanbrugh demonstrated a feeling for Gothic form, but it was in the second quarter of the eighteenth century that "Rococo Gothick" had its beginning, when William Kent and Sanderson Miller introduced the use of Gothic details in a purely decorative manner, adapted and applied to classical forms.[5] The ornamental use of Gothic motifs, often borrowed from ecclesiastical buildings, in an elegant and fanciful way became a lively fashion in the light-hearted spirit of the prevalent Rococo mode. Gothic details and adaptations began to be published in books, like Batty Langley's attempt to reduce Gothic to orders and to introduce "improved" versions of "modern Gothick," and Thomas Chippendale's adaptations of motifs for furniture design.[6] The delicate, whimsical "Rococo Gothick" appeared in effects created for landscape gardens—temples, umbrellos, and sham ruins—in several churches, and in a number of remarkable country houses, such as Sir Roger Newdigate's Arbury Hall and Horace Walpole's influential Strawberry Hill.

Knowledge of the Gothic gradually increased through the study and restoration of medieval buildings, and architects gained experience in working with the style. They used its details with somewhat greater accuracy and exploited its forms for the dramatic quality, as is seen particularly in the works of James Wyatt at Lee Priory, Ashridge, and the extravaganza Fonthill Abbey. Toward the end of the eighteenth century interest in the style took a new, important turn. In the scenic hills of western England and Wales the aesthetic theory of the Picturesque was formulated.[7] Its writers stressed that landscapes should be viewed as they are in the works of painters like Claude Lorrain, Salvator Rosa, and Jacob van Ruisdael, that landscape gardens should seek similar pictorial effects, and that country houses should be designed as a visual unity with their natural settings. Admiring especially the irregularity, drama, and variety of wild scenery, the writers emphasized that houses for such "Picturesque" surroundings should have irregularities of form, composition, and feature, with variety, rough textures, contrasts of light and shade, movement, drama, and even surprise. These qualities were found in the Gothic style, which became the chief architectural expression of the Picturesque point of view.

Richard Payne Knight's Downton (1774–1778) was the prototype of the Picturesque castellated mansion. Many architects followed his example in the early nineteenth century, and the designs of John Nash were especially scenic. Interest also developed in country houses of more moderate size (villas) and in ornamental cottages (*cottages ornés*), which were built for rustic effects on large estates and emulated for parsonages and other modest dwellings. Numerous books of suitable designs were published from 1790 on into the 1830s; often beautifully delineated and usually more or less Gothic in style, the designs became important in stimulating and influencing Gothic as a style for country houses in America. Publications illustrating ancient Gothic buildings likewise increased in number, accuracy, and detail and were used in America as source material for revival buildings and decoration. England's Gothic Revival was stimulated in the 1820s by the erection of many churches under the Act of 1818 (called Commissioners' Churches), but even more important impetus came from the rebuilding of the Houses of Parliament (1836–1860), after a disastrous fire destroyed the earlier buildings.

In the late 1830s and 1840s the nature of the Gothic Revival in England changed—from pictorial and associational to structural and archeological. With this change the revival reached maturity; its romantic youth was over. Augustus Welby Northmore Pugin and the Ecclesiologists insisted on strict archeological correctness, on logical, "truthful" construction with no "shams" and only such ornament as was related to structure.[8] For their models they turned from the previously favored late Perpendicular period to the earlier periods of medieval Gothic. Primarily concerned with church architecture, this Early Victorian Gothic also changed secular building toward more solid construction, a heavier aspect, and simpler detailing. With midcentury influences from the Continent, including John Ruskin's predilection for rich Venetian polychromy, the movement evolved toward the eclecticism and bold originality of High Victorian Gothic.

The Gothic Revival was slow to reach America. Evidences of the Gothic taste in colonial America are rare—as widely scattered as the ogee-arched porch of Gunston Hall in Fairfax County, Virginia, ceiling details of the Miles Brewton House (and probably its uncertainly-dated, battlemented coach house) in Charleston, a Boston mantelpiece, and Philadelphia Chippendale furniture derived from the *Director*. By the end of the century a few churches were embellished with pointed arches, sharp pinnacles, and, occasionally, clustered columns, as at Trinity Church in New York (1789). In the first quarter of the nineteenth century the use of Gothic detailing for churches gradually increased, and in the 1820s the Gothic gained momentum as an accepted style. Builders of Episcopalian churches especially found the Gothic appropriate, probably spurred by the Commissioners' churches in England. As early as 1807 the English-trained architect Benjamin H. Latrobe had designed handsome fan vaults for his Gothic Philadelphia Bank, and by 1830 Gothic features appeared on a variety of buildings—on Masonic halls in Philadelphia and New York, on prisons in Boston, Philadelphia, and Auburn, New York, on a fishing clubhouse on the Schuylkill River, at Kenyon College in Ohio, and on the state capitol of Georgia.

Before the 1830s only a few American houses are known to have been built in the style. For Sedgeley, William Crammond's Philadelphia country house (1799), Latrobe grafted pointed arches, labels, and eaves ornamentation onto a classical shape, while the façade of John Dorsey's Philadelphia town house (ca. 1810) displayed crisply decorative detailing (no. 190). On Talcott Mountain near Hartford, Connecticut, Daniel Wadsworth built a Gothic cottage and a country house with long pointed windows sometime before 1819, while about 1825 Turner Camac's delightful cottage appeared at the edge of settled Philadelphia, built in the picturesque Rural Gothic style with a steep roof, twin front gables, and decorative ornaments along the eaves.

During the 1830s an increasing number of significant Gothic and gothicizing ventures were undertaken at widely scattered sites. In 1832 young Robert Gilmor, who had recently returned from England, began his gently castellated Glen Ellen near Baltimore. Designed by Ithiel Town and Alexander Jackson Davis, the delicately detailed Glen Ellen reflected Gilmor's fascination with Strawberry Hill and Abbotsford. Two years later Davis made his first design for a Hudson River villa "in the English Collegiate Style" (planned for Robert Donaldson, but never built) with an irregular shape and a fifty-foot octagonal tower, "suited to scenery of a picturesque character."[9] About the same time James Fenimore Cooper and Washington Irving, both recently returned from long sojourns abroad, were busy at work; Cooper began to gothicize his Otsego Hall (no. 184) on the frontier of central New York state, while Irving and the English artist George Harvey transformed a simple Dutch cottage on the Hudson into the picturesque Sunnyside (no. 170). At a bend of the Kennebec River in Maine rose Robert H. Gardiner's Oaklands (1835–1836), designed by Richard Upjohn to resemble a handsome Tudor manor house, while overlooking the New Haven, Connecticut, harbor, Sidney M. Stone planned a stiffly castellated villa (no. 178) for Gerard H. Hallock (1836). Sometime in the 1830s Thomas Ludlow built a charming cottage on the lower Hudson at Yonkers, and on Long Island Sound near New Rochelle the Reverend Robert Bolton built his towered Priory in 1838.

In June 1838 Davis released two thin numbers of his *Rural Residences*, the first book that attempted to encourage in America a rural architecture suited to the natural landscape. He praised "the picturesque Cottages and Villas of England" and deplored "the bald and uninteresting aspect of our houses . . . [and the] defects . . . not only in the style of the house but in the want of connexion with its site."[10] Among his Gothic designs he included Robert Donaldson's board-and-batten gate lodge at Blithewood, near Barrytown, New York (1836), the prototype of the American Gothic cottage. In 1838 Davis also designed several Gothic villas and cottages, two of which, at Tarrytown, New York, were to be particularly influential: Henry Sheldon's Millbrook, in board-and-batten cottage style, and the "Country Mansion in Pointed Style" for William Paulding and his son Philip R. Paulding, a picturesque blend of *cottage orné* and castellation, and the nucleus of the later Lyndhurst.

Through the 1840s the Gothic Revival style gained rapidly in popularity; it flourished at midcentury, had already begun to decline by the outbreak of the Civil War, and lingered on into the 1870s. Strongly influential in the rising popularity of the style in the 1840s were the writings of Andrew Jackson Downing, America's first important landscape gardener. His brief life (1815–1852) was spent in Newburgh, New York, where in 1839 he built for his bride a Tudor villa, overlooking a spectacular view of the Hudson River and its mountains. An ardent protagonist of the Picturesque theory of landscape gardening and rural architecture, he presented it lucidly to Americans in simplified terms and appealed to the pride and ambition of his countrymen to improve their country properties with "smiling lawns and tasteful cottages."[11]

Tudor Gothic—and its simplified version that he called the English cottage style or Rural Gothic—was his favorite mode, and he urged it upon Americans as most suited to their own natural scenery and country life:

> To the man of taste, there is no style which presents greater attractions, being at once rich in picturesque beauty, and harmonious in connection with the surrounding forms of vegetation.... the Rural Gothic, the lines of which point upwards, in the pyramidal gables, tall clusters of chimneys, finials, and the several other portions of its varied outline, harmonizes easily with the tall trees, the tapering masses of foliage, or the surrounding hills; and while it is seldom or never misplaced in spirited rural scenery, it gives character and picturesque expression to many landscapes entirely devoid of that quality.[12]

Rural Gothic aroused associations "of a highly *romantic* and *poetical* nature,"[13] while it also was adaptable to convenient interior planning and easily susceptible to addition. Downing, neither architect nor artist, turned for assistance to A. J. Davis. For more than a decade Davis drew most of the appealing illustrations of villas and cottages in Downing's works. Some of the illustrations were Davis's own designs, a few were by other architects, and many were the joint work of Downing and Davis, for which the relative responsibility varied from design to design.

The cottages and cottage-style villas that evolved—now often called "Downing cottages"—were American versions of the *cottage orné*. Decorative features enlivened their aspect, and irregularities broke the severity of their outline, even when the cottages were not asymmetrical. Typical embellishments included sharp gables trimmed with carved vergeboards, finials, and pendants; high chimney-pots; diamond-paned casement windows crowned with labels or sometimes arched and filled with tracery; delicately crested bay and oriel windows; and ornamental verandas with decorative supports, spandrels, and crestings. Cottage designs interpreted in wood were particularly original when novel board-and-batten siding enhanced their surface texture, verticality, and rusticity. In the hands of experienced architects, the effects were carefully orchestrated and controlled. In Davis's designs for Henry Delamater at Rhinebeck, New York (1844), and for William J. Rotch at New Bedford,

Massachusetts (1845), the central gables reach a dramatic height and the ornamental detailing is beautifully conceived. In Joseph C. Wells's Roseland (no. 187), built for Henry C. Bowen at Woodstock, Connecticut (1846), the array of dormers is charming. The delightful gate lodge (now gone), built for James Winslow south of Poughkeepsie, New York, and the board-and-batten cottage villa designed for Henry Ten Eyck at Cazenovia, New York (1847), are two fine examples by unknown architects.

In that period of romantic sensitivity to natural scenery and of avid interest in horticulture, Downing's books became widely popular and influential. Other authors followed his example to produce many "pattern books" of country-house designs. Local builders and carpenters adapted the designs and worked out their own variations, even when it meant only adding a few details to embellish symmetrical house shapes. The opportunity of decking verandas, gables, and eaves with "gingerbread" stimulated a vernacular expression of folk art that blossomed in the invention of a great variety of fanciful creations. The results are seen across the country: the lacy veiling on the "Wedding Cake House" at Kennebunk, Maine; the colorful fringes on Oak Bluffs cottages at Martha's Vineyard, Massachusetts; and the whimsical trimmings on houses in the Middle West, in Colorado mining towns, and on the Pacific coast. Gothic cottages brought a touch of fantasy to the American scene, and the ones that still remain exert an irresistible charm.

With towers, turrets, and battlements, the Gothic villas were highly pictorial. They were usually sited on hillsides overlooking splendid views of woods and water. Their grounds were carefully landscaped to capture picturesque effects and were often embellished with gatehouses, coach houses, greenhouses, and gazebos in the Gothic mode. At first Gothic motifs were merely applied to traditional boxy shapes—a few arched doors and windows, some labels, perhaps a battlemented parapet or even an appended tower. But, from the late 1830s on, as the style developed under the influence of the Picturesque theory, emphasis shifted toward irregularity and complexity of design, toward diversity of shapes and asymmetry of composition, with divergencies in height and feature to break the skyline. Great variety resulted, from the tight compactness of Font Hill's six interlocking towers, built for actor Edwin Forrest and overlooking the Hudson at Yonkers, New York (1847), to the loose sprawl of C. Tyler Longstreet's castle in Syracuse, designed by James Renwick, Jr. (1851). A villa could appear open and informal, like Afton Villa created for David Barrow at Saint Francisville, Louisiana (1849), or severely dignified, like Staunton Hill in Charlotte County, Virginia, constructed for Charles Bruce by John E. Johnson (1848); or it could combine cottage informality with a formal block, as in Kingscote, designed for George Noble Jones at Newport, Rhode Island, by Richard Upjohn (1841). In the prosperous 1850s the size of country houses tended to increase and the ornamentation to become more elaborate. At times in the late 1850s and the 1860s the detailing became heavier and the effect more stolid, and occasionally the polychromy of Venetian Gothic appeared, as in Edward Newton Perkins's Pinebank built by Sturgis and Brigham at Jamaica Plain, Massachusetts (1870).

A number of the most graceful and picturesque villas were designed by Davis, who had a fine scenic sense and an eye for dramatic effects. Even as a youth, he had spent "hours in puzzling over the plan of some ancient castle of romance, arranging the trap doors, subterraneous passages and drawbridges,"[14] and the only two houses that he designed for himself were both Gothic, a cottage for his mother and his own mountain-top lodge. His love for the Gothic was not just a personal romantic response. It was an architect's realization of style suited to setting: of vertical lines, broken silhouettes, and irregular forms in harmony with a wild natural terrain, of boldness and drama where nature herself was only half tamed. In Gothic, Davis found the fascination of new forms and motifs for experimentation, released from the rigid symmetry of the classical box.

"I want some handsome villa of *yours* to put in my new work—shall it be Kents, or Harolds [i.e. Harral's] or what?" Downing wrote Davis on March 5, 1849. "It has occurred to me that my old favorite the 'James villa' which hangs in your room would perhaps be as good a thing as can be produced by any living or dead man!"[15] This unexecuted 1841 design was modified for a number of his smaller villas, including Hurst-Pierrepont for Edwards Pierrepont at Garrison, New York, in 1863. It was symmetrical, but as Davis developed his skill in the composition of masses, his larger villas became increasingly asymmetrical. The early Kenwood (no. 187), built for Joel Rathbone south of Albany, New York (1842), was a lively assemblage of projections and vertical accents and had one of Davis's first open, radiating plans. In many of his designs the elements rose dramatically in rhythmic crescendo to a climax near the center, as in his suburban villa for William C. H. Waddell (no. 191) on New York City's Murray Hill (1844). In Henry K. Harral's Walnut Wood (no. 185) at Bridgeport, Connecticut (1846), he reversed the Waddell pattern and added an ornamental veranda. Some of his villas were dominated by a bold stair tower like the one at Ingleside, designed for Edwin B. Strange in Dobbs Ferry, New York (1854), and a few, set in "wild and romantic scenery,"[16] were built of rough-cut stone and castellated, like John J. Herrick's Ericstan above Tarrytown, New York (1855), and Joseph Howard's Castlewood in Llewellyn Park, West Orange, New Jersey (1858). For Philip St. George Cocke's Belmead on the James River in Virginia (1845), Davis created a handsome Tudor tower. Twenty years later he developed this tower pattern in the great tall tower of Lyndhurst (no. 189), when in 1865–1867 he enlarged Paulding's Knoll for George Merritt in an intricately balanced composition, the culmination of his Gothic designing.

The Gothic Revival as a style for domestic architecture developed first as a mode for country houses, but when the style became fashionable, it spread to cities, where Gothic features appeared on various types of urban dwellings. Some were free-standing structures like the handsome Green-Meldrim house in Savannah, Georgia (1856), or rectories of Gothic churches such as the elegant one of Grace Church in New York City designed by James Renwick, Jr. (1847). Large attached town houses also stood within rows beside houses of other styles, as, for example, the fine houses of James Lenox and his sister on Fifth Avenue and of James W. Gerard on Gramercy Park, New York City. Numerous more modest row houses had Gothic detailing on doorways, windows, and cornices. A long block of Gothic houses was built on New York City's West Twentieth Street, and on Fifth Avenue at Forty-second Street facing the Croton Reservoir rose the remarkable "House of Mansions" (no. 193) designed by Davis (1858), a block of "eleven dwellings being combined as in one palace."[17]

The cold discomfort of a medieval fortified castle—or even of a Tudor manor house—held little attraction for a nineteenth-century homeowner. The interiors of Gothic Revival houses, like their exteriors, made no attempt to follow medieval prototypes; Horace Walpole had already stated the attitude in the eighteenth century when he remarked, "I did not mean to make my house so Gothic as to exclude convenience."[18] Indeed, the asymmetry of Picturesque villas afforded unprecedented opportunities for the imaginative planning of interior layouts, based on convenience or whim; rooms of diverse shapes might be variously disposed, and unexpected nooks, passageways, or even a secret door might be included. Staircases no longer dominated a formal, symmetrical plan, but might be shunted to an inconspicuous spot; spiral stairs might wind their way up a tower, or a great stairhall might rise through two stories, as at Walnut Wood, where giant arches terminated in masks of Dante, Shakespeare, Washington, and other greats of literature and history.

To hint of medieval antiquity—and to exploit the decorative possibilities of the style—Gothic detailing of varying elaboration was employed, much of it executed in plaster. More elegant mansions boasted archways, traceried doors and windows framed by colonnettes and crowned by labels, stained glass, cornices of small battlements or Tudor flowers, clustered columns, carved paneling, foliated spandrels, ribbed and vaulted ceilings with bosses, corbels, carvings, and pendants, and mantels displaying characteristic motifs. The interior finish of the cottages was often quite simple, but they, too, had a special air, even if only from the inside effect of the lattice windows, the projecting bays, and the steeply pitched gables and dormers.

Libraries, associated with medieval learning, often had richly carved bookcases and elaborate ceilings. Splendid Gothic libraries sometimes occurred in houses of other styles: Bishop George Washington Doane's elegant library at Riverside in Burlington, New Jersey (an early Italianate villa by John Notman, ca. 1839), the handsome octagonal library of William B. Astor at Rokeby, near Barrytown, New York, and the ornately vaulted library in David S. Kennedy's town house on Fifth Avenue, New York City, are three examples.

Probably none of the American Gothic Revival houses were furnished entirely in the Gothic taste, but the intimate relationship that exists between architecture and the decorative arts is strikingly demonstrated by the way in which Gothic motifs permeated every aspect of the decorative field. No attempt was made to reproduce actual medieval furniture models; few examples were known, even fewer were available in illustration, and almost none were suited to ideas of nineteenth-century comfort. Medieval architectural motifs were adapted and applied to contemporary furniture forms as ornament. At first Gothic motifs were used tentatively, conjointly with classical or other stylistic motifs; later they played a more dominant role in design and exerted an influence on form, for the use of such elements as pinnacles, finials, and arches often gave an architectural quality to furniture shapes. English books and the foreign training of craftsmen afforded inspiration, but the objects produced in this country attained a distinctly American character. Rococo "Gothick" motifs had appeared on Chippendale furniture in eighteenth-century America. Arcaded tracery frequently graced neoclassical bookcases and secretaries, and a few motifs appeared in the work of such early nineteenth-century craftsmen as the Irish-born cabinetmaker Joseph B. Barry, who worked in

Philadelphia.[19] In the 1830s the style was increasingly employed, and it reached the height of its popularity and complexity in the 1840s and 1850s. As interpreted by diverse makers, the furniture was produced in intriguing variety and encompassed most types of pieces. It was unusual to have furniture designed by an architect, like that of A. J. Davis, whose documented designs are highly individualistic and often depart from cabinetmakers' formulae. Gothic furniture seems to have been especially fashionable for libraries and halls, and many nineteenth-century houses that were mainly furnished in a different style kept up with fashion by acquiring an item or two in the Gothic taste.

Gothic motifs appeared everywhere: on porcelain vases and pottery covered jars, on lacy glass compotes and pickle bottles. Lighting fixtures, silver, fabrics, needlework, and wallpaper displayed pointed arches, crockets, trefoils, and quatrefoils; these motifs were also cast into iron for garden furniture, stoves, birdhouses, footscrapers, and numerous other articles.

Gothic Revival houses and their furnishings were by no means the only evidences, or even the chief evidences, of the style in America. It was used in designs for almost every type of building. Gothic especially became, and long remained, the dominant mode for churches. Passing through a succession of phases, the use of Gothic persisted in architecture far into the twentieth century and has left a considerable mark not only in churches but in such important skyscrapers as the Woolworth Building and the Chicago Tribune Tower, where its vertical qualities give emphasis to the soaring height.

In its Romantic period the Gothic Revival style was a wondrously creative force. Breaking the absolute dominance of classicism, it stimulated a new inventiveness; transcending the limitations of symmetry, it opened the way for freedom of design. The reintroduction of medieval forms brought great enrichment and a touch of fantasy to the American scene, and it had a strongly creative impact on the decorative arts. Today, in the midst of twentieth-century austerity and standardization, the Gothic Revival furniture and other decorative objects from that period retain an amazing freshness and appeal that enchant the eye and excite the imagination.

JANE B. DAVIES

1. Andrew Jackson Downing, "A Few Words on Rural Architecture," *The Horticulturist and Journal of Rural Art and Rural Taste* V (July 1850), 10, reprinted in his *Rural Essays* (New York: G. P. Putnam and Co., 1853), 207.

2. Sir Walter Scott, *The Lady of the Lake* (Edinburgh: John Ballantyne and Co., 1810), 4.

3. The term "Gothic Revival" is often used in a restricted sense, chiefly by scholars in England, for the mature phases of the revival from about 1840 on, with the earlier phases designated by the eighteenth-century spelling "Gothick." In America this distinction has generally not been made, and the term is usually used in the broader sense to cover the earlier phases also. The Gothic Revival is also called "Neo-Gothic," especially in reference to the movement on an international scope, since an equivalent of "Gothic Revival" has not been used in languages other than English. The term "Gothic" itself was a misnomer, which troubled men in the eighteenth and early nineteenth centuries before scholarship uncovered the origins of the medieval Gothic style, and numerous efforts were made to substitute other terms for this medieval architecture.

4. Alexander Jackson Davis, "Address," in an unpaged manuscript portfolio entitled "Rural Residences, etc.," Avery Architectural Library, Columbia University, New York, Davis Collection I, no. G1. This unfinished draft presumably was intended as an introduction for an edition of Davis's work by that title (see notes 9 and 10).

5. Tom Tower (1681–1682) at Christ Church, Oxford, was Wren's best known Gothic essay; Vanbrugh's own castle at

Greenwich (ca. 1717) recalled the form of a medieval fortress; Kent's decorative Gothic at Esher Lodge (between 1729 and 1739) and elsewhere was immediately influential. These architects worked chiefly in the classical tradition, but the amateur architect Miller created his most interesting work in the Gothic mode. Especially notable was his new hall at Lacock Abbey (1753-1755).

6. Batty Langley, *Gothic Architecture, Improved by Rules and Proportions* (London: Taylor, [1742]), and Thomas Chippendale, *The Gentleman and Cabinet-maker's Director* (London: The author, 1754).

7. For a discussion of this theory, see Christopher Hussey, *The Picturesque: Studies in a Point of View* (London and New York: G. P. Putnam's Sons, 1927).

8. The most influential works of Pugin (an intensely religious Roman Catholic convert) were: *Contrasts* (Salisbury: For the Author, 1836), *The True Principles of Pointed or Christian Architecture* (London: John Weale, 1841), and *An Apology for the Revival of Christian Architecture in England* (London: John Weale, 1843). Many of his architectural principles were shared by the Anglican Cambridge Camden Society (later the Ecclesiological Society) and were promoted in its periodical, *The Ecclesiologist*, which began publication in 1841.

9. Alexander Jackson Davis, *Rural Residences, etc. Consisting of Designs . . . for Cottages, Farm-houses, Villas and Village Churches . . . Published . . . with a View to the Improvement of American Country Architecture* (New York: To Be Had of the Architect, 1837), unpaged letterpress facing the lithograph of the villa. The house was planned for a site at Fishkill Landing (now Beacon), New York. Davis, Downing, and others at that time were inexact and inconsistent in the terms that they used for various types of Gothic, and their choice of features was little concerned with distinctions of period.

10. Davis, *Rural Residences*, from the introductory "Advertisement" (unpaged). The publication was projected to comprise six parts, but only two parts appeared, both in June 1838, despite the title-page date of 1837.

11. Andrew Jackson Downing, *The Architecture of Country Houses* (New York: D. Appleton and Co., 1850), v.

12. Andrew Jackson Downing, *A Treatise on the Theory and Practice of Landscape Gardening, Adapted to North America; With a View to the Improvement of Country Residences* (2d ed.; New York and London: Wiley and Putnam, 1844), 374; as quoted, this passage is very slightly revised from that of the first edition (New York and London: Wiley and Putnam, 1841), 329-330.

13. Downing, *A Treatise on . . . Landscape Gardening* (1841), 330.

14. William Dunlap, *History of the Rise and Progress of the Arts of Design in the United States* (New York: George P. Scott and Co., 1834), II, 409.

15. Downing to Davis, March 5, 1849, Metropolitan Museum of Art, New York, A. J. Davis Collection, file box Letters and Papers. The design was made for John B. James for a site on the Hudson near Rhinecliff, New York; the original watercolor is in the Avery Architectural Library, Columbia University, New York. It was published as Design XXX, "A Villa in the Pointed Style," in Downing's *The Architecture of Country Houses*, 338-342. Dates of Davis's designs as given in this essay are generally the year of the inception of the design.

16. Downing, *A Treatise on . . . Landscape Gardening* (1841), 339. Downing felt that this was the only type of setting for which Castellated Gothic was appropriate.

17. Prospectus: "For Sale on Moderate Terms: the Block of Dwelling Houses upon Murray Hill" [New York, 1859]. The description was written by Davis, at least in part (Avery Architectural Library, Columbia University, New York, Day Book, v. 2, p. 150, August 30, 1859). The view was also undoubtedly based on a drawing by Davis.

18. Horace Walpole, *A Description of the Villa . . . at Strawberry-Hill* (Strawberry-Hill: Printed by Thomas Kirgate, 1784), iii. First edition was privately printed in 1774.

19. Barry advertised furniture in the Gothic style as early as 1810 (see Robert T. Trump, "Joseph B. Barry, Philadelphia cabinetmaker," *Antiques* CVII [January 1975], 162).

The Gothic Revival Style in America, 1830–1870

NOTE: *All dimensions of objects in this exhibition are given in inches followed by centimeters in parentheses. An asterisk (*) denotes objects significant enough to be included in the catalogue but which could not be transported to Texas for the exhibition. Where shortened bibliographic information appears in footnotes, full citations are provided in the bibliography at the end of the catalogue. Where applicable, the last number given after the lender's name is the lender's accession number.*

1   Side Chair
    United States, ca. 1835–1850
    Mahogany
    H. 37¼ (94.6) W. 17¾ (45.1) D. 17½ (44.45)
    Mr. Jay E. Cantor

Mahogany Restauration-style side chairs with slip seats, console legs, shaped splats, and stiles flowing into arched crest rails were typical features of America's late Empire period. This chair graphically illustrates the transition between the Restauration style and the Gothic Revival. Gothic arches, a quatrefoil, and a finial have been grafted onto the upper section of a basically Restauration form to create a flamboyant Gothic back. This particular chair is marked with a Roman "XIIII" [sic] on the upper surface of its front seat rail. It is said to have come from an unidentified Brooklyn, New York, home.

KSH

2   Side Chair
    Alexander and Frederick Roux (active partnership ca. 1847–1849)
    New York, New York, 1848
    Oak
    H. 33½ (85.09) W. 18 (45.72) D. 17 (43.18)
    Mr. Lee B. Anderson

This Gothicized version of the Restauration side chair, apparently based on a French prototype, is a form that was made in at least several variations by a number of different cabinetmakers. It is rare when one can pinpoint Gothic Revival examples as to maker and date, but the stenciled label of "A. and F. Roux at 479 Broadway, New York" not only gives us this information but also indicates the date, 1848, the only year the partnership was located at that address.

DBW

3   Side Chair
    United States, ca. 1850
    Mahogany
    H. 33¾ (85.73) W. 18 (45.72) D. 17¾ (45.40)
    The Brooklyn Museum, Brooklyn, New York
    56.X.30.1

Simple framed chairs with upholstered seats, console legs, and flat crest rails contained by posts are holdovers from the 1830s Restauration style.[1] How-

1

2

3

4

6

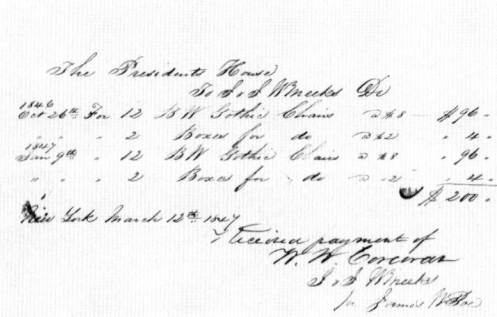

5

7

ever, this chair, which is part of a set of two armchairs and three side chairs, has added two new elements: long, ogee arches and trefoils. This basic design, varying in degrees of quality and emanating from more than one shop, was popular from Washington, D.C., to the Hudson River Valley. Four black walnut chairs now in the White House are thought to be among the two dozen sold there by John and Joseph W. Meeks in 1846–1847 (see nos. 4 and 176); Washington Irving used six similar, but less refined, mahogany chairs at Sunnyside. Alexander and Frederick Roux also made such lancet-back side chairs, producing a sophisticated, labeled, oak example in 1848.[2]   KSH

1. Celia Jackson Otto, *American Furniture of the Nineteenth Century*, 274.
2. Helen Comstock, *American Furniture: Seventeenth, Eighteenth, and Nineteenth Century Styles*, 292–293; and *19th-Century America: Furniture and Other Decorative Arts*, no. 99.

4   Side Chair
    Attributed to John and Joseph W. Meeks (active partnership ca. 1836–1859)
    New York, New York, ca. 1846–1847
    Black walnut
    H. 34¼ (87) W. 17 (43.18) D. 17½ (44.45)
    Mr. Graham Williford, Fairfield, Texas

5   Payment Voucher from the U.S. General Treasury Account to J. and J. W. Meeks, 1846–1847
    Records of Receipts and Expenditures of the U.S. Treasury Account, Account 97.137, Voucher No. 45
    Ink on paper
    H. 4⅞ (12.38) W. 7¾ (19.69)
    The National Archives, Washington, D.C.

During the administration of President James K. Polk new chairs were required for the White House. His staff chose light, comfortable, moderately priced side chairs in the fashionable Restauration-Gothic style. Later, President Abraham Lincoln used them in the Cabinet Room (no. 176), and the four remaining chairs at the White House now grace the Lincoln Bedroom.

This chair is ascribed to the original White House set. It was purchased from a descendant of the Hazard family, which traditionally believes that this chair and its mate were given to their family by President Andrew Johnson. The chair probably was among a set of twenty-four "B[lack?] W[alnut?] Gothic Chairs" costing $192 (plus $8 shipping), which were purchased from John and Joseph W. Meeks in 1846 and 1847 (no. 5).   KSH

6 Side Chair and Armchair†
   Probably New England or New York, ca. 1840–1850
   Mahogany veneer, mahogany, poplar
   H. 32¼ (81.92) W. 18 (45.72) D. 16 (40.64)
   Stowe-Day Foundation, Hartford, Connecticut   68.124

In overall design these chairs are very similar to others of the period, but a modest point on the crest rail is a new feature. Two of a set of four side chairs and two armchairs, they descended from Henry Ward Beecher (1811–1887), the fiery abolitionist preacher of Brooklyn's Plymouth Congregational Church and brother of Harriet Beecher Stowe. It was Roseland's (no. 186) Henry C. Bowen who was a founder of Plymouth Church and who invited Beecher to preach there.[1]   KSH

1. Polly Rabinowitz, "Life at Roseland: Bowens and Holts," 7–8.
† Not illustrated.

7 Armchair
   Attributed to Anthony G. Quervelle (d. 1856)
   Philadelphia, Pennsylvania, ca. 1830–1856
   Walnut, pine
   H. 38½ (97.79) W. 19 (48.26) D. 22 (55.88)
   Mr. Lee B. Anderson

The scrolled cross with central diamond-shaped boss lends a medieval heraldic character to the back of this armchair, perhaps echoed in the eyes of the nineteenth-century viewer by the spiral turnings of the front legs. The timid Gothic peak at the top of the back differentiates this chair from similar Restauration forms. A surviving bill of sale indicates the chair was made by Anthony G. Quervelle for William Pennington, governor of New Jersey (1837–1843).[1]   DBW

1. Robert C. Smith, "The Furniture of Anthony G. Quervelle, Part V: Sofas, Chairs, and Beds," *Antiques* CV (March 1974), 520.

8 Armchair
   Philadelphia, Pennsylvania, ca. 1830
   Maple veneer, maple
   H. 44½ (113.03) W. 26¾ (67.95) D. 18 (45.72)
   Mr. and Mrs. James Biddle

This curule-based armchair with whimsical castellated crest and crocketed stiles is veneered with the same highly figured maple that was utilized on several Empire sofas and a set of chairs installed at Nicholas Biddle's Andalusia following Thomas U. Walter's remodeling in the 1830s. Walter had sketched a Gothic ruin for Biddle's neoclassical house (no. 183), and undoubtedly a chair with mixed classical and medieval details did not seem incongruous.   DBW

8

9 Armchair
   Philadelphia, Pennsylvania, ca. 1840–1850
   Oak, tulipwood
   H. 45⅝ (115.89) W. 21¾ (55.25) D. 19⅝ (49.85)
   Mr. and Mrs. James Biddle

In the 1840s a small Gothic Revival cottage was added to the complex of buildings at Nicholas Biddle's country seat, Andalusia (no. 183). At that time several pieces of Gothic furniture were purchased by the Biddles for use in the cottage. Included was this armchair and a matching bench (no. 52). Octagonal, pillar-like legs and cusped arches lend an architectural flavor that is repeated in the arms of the chair. A flamboyant finial crowning the back contrasts with the otherwise austere aspect of this example.   DBW

9

10

11

10 Side Chair

Designed by Alexander Jackson Davis (1803–1892)
New York, New York, ca. 1845–1850
Walnut
H. 39¼ (99.70) W. 18⅝ (47.31) D. (at seat rail) 17 (43.18)
Museum of the City of New York, gift of Joseph B. Davis   35.257.67

11 Drawing

Alexander Jackson Davis (1803–1892)
New York, New York, ca. 1845–1850
Pencil on paper
H. 8⅞ (22.5) W. 5⅞ (14)
Avery Architectural Library, Columbia University, New York, New York, A. J. Davis Collection   C 1-1-n

Alexander Jackson Davis's chair design, while remarkably simple, adequately conveys a Gothic sense through its three undulating arches, which terminate at an attractively crocketed crest rail. Despite a variation in the back, similarity to a Davis sketch for another cloven-foot chair (no. 11) clearly establishes the origin of this example. Further, the chair was given to its present owner by Davis's son, Joseph Beale Davis.   KSH

12 Side Chair

Designed by Alexander Jackson Davis (1803–1892)
New York, New York, ca. 1841
Oak with cane seat
H. 37 (93.98) W. 18½ (49.99) D. 17½ (44.45)
Lyndhurst, National Trust for Historic Preservation, Tarrytown, New York
            NT 64.25.9 a

While other wheel-back chairs hint at medieval origins (nos. 45 and 46), this chair, one of a pair designed by Alexander Jackson Davis, blends two direct medieval allusions in a form designed for the "saloon" at Philip R. Paulding's Lyndhurst (no. 189). Not only is the back consciously fashioned after a cathedral's rose window, but in one preliminary sketch for this chair, Davis labeled it a "Catherine Wheelback, No. 43."[1] St. Catherine of Alexandria was the saint who was martyred on a wheel. As with most of Davis's designs, it is difficult, if not impossible, to ascribe a maker to it. He worked with both Richard Byrne of White Plains, New York, and William Burns of the New York firm favored by Andrew Jackson Downing: Burns and Tranque (or Trainque).[2] Although Davis's papers do include an entry stating that "R. Byrne, cabinetmaker, White Plains, made Paulding's chairs," it is impossible to say that this wheel-back chair, or any given chair, at Lyndhurst is the example to which he refers.[3]   KSH

1. The drawing is in the collection of the Museum of the City of New York (35.257.41). It was a gift to the museum from the designer's son, Joseph Beale Davis.
2. The question of Davis's cabinetmakers is compounded by a conflicting memoir written by Joseph Beale Davis. The problem is addressed in Stanley Mallach, "Gothic Furniture Designs by Alexander Jackson Davis," 128–137. Andrew Jackson Downing credited Burns and Tranque with the following: "The most correct Gothic furniture that we have yet seen executed in this country . . . ." in *The Architecture of Country Houses*, 440.
3. Mallach, "Gothic Furniture Designs," 136.

13 Hall Chair

Design attributed to Alexander Jackson Davis (1803–1892)
New York, New York, ca. 1841
Oak with cane seat
H. 42½ (107.32) W. 15 (38.10) D. 17¾ (45.09)
Lyndhurst, National Trust for Historic Preservation, Tarrytown, New York
            NT 64.25.189 a

Stylistic similarities between this delicate chair, which is one of a pair, and other known Alexander Jackson Davis side and hall chairs (nos. 10 and 12) form the basis for the Davis attribution here. Surviving Davis manuscript material indicates that he designed at least fifty different furnishings for Philip R. Paulding between 1841 and 1847,[1] and this chair may be one of them.   KSH

1. Stanley Mallach, "Gothic Furniture Designs by Alexander Jackson Davis," 123.

14   Side Chair
　　Design attributed to Alexander Jackson Davis
　　　(1803–1892)
　　New York, New York, ca. 1841–1847
　　Oak
　　H. 45 (114.30) W. 18¾ (47.53) D. 18 (45.72)
　　Lyndhurst, National Trust for Historic Preservation, Tarrytown, New York
　　　　　　　　　　　　　　NT 64. 25.4 b

Because so many other chairs at Lyndhurst are documented Alexander Jackson Davis pieces, this chair may be associated with his work as well. Certainly its cloven feet are similar to those on another documented Davis chair (no. 10) and are seemingly unique in nineteenth-century American Gothic Revival furniture, although Augustus Welby Northmore Pugin used them repeatedly in his furniture designs. This particular example replicates a medieval chair as correctly as any seen to date.   KSH

15   Armchair
　　Designed by Alexander Jackson Davis (1803–1892)
　　New York, New York, ca. 1841–1866
　　Oak
　　H. 45½ (115.57) W. 20 (50.80) D. 21 (53.34)
　　Lyndhurst, National Trust for Historic Preservation, Tarrytown, New York
　　　　　　　　　　　　　　NT 64.25.684 a

Tucked in one corner of an Alexander Jackson Davis drawing, "Interior in a simple Gothic Style," is a version of this chair, one of twelve made for (and still in) the dining room at Lyndhurst.[1] The design of this chair is very similar to a design that Davis made for chairs in Samuel E. Lyon's White Plains home and almost identical to a Davis sketch for a Lyndhurst chair.[2] The chair's deeply carved crockets, spandrels, and arms and well-articulated trefoil drops make it an especially good interpretation of a functional, but interesting, Gothic armchair. The shallow incising on the top of its crestrail and the lance-like darts carved into each leg are later modes, indicating that the chair may have been updated, if not made, during George Merritt's years at Lyndhurst in the

12

14

13

15

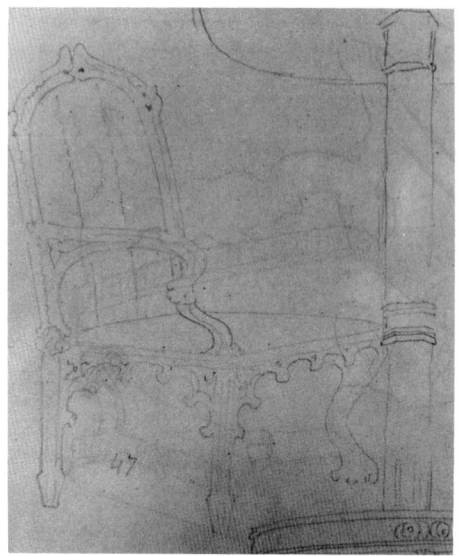

16

1860s. If the chair had been fabricated in the 1860s from an earlier drawing, it may explain why no record of it exists in the Davis papers under Merritt's entries.[3]   KSH

1. Andrew Jackson Downing, *The Architecture of Country Houses*, 383.
2. Alexander Jackson Davis, Papers, Avery Library, Columbia University, New York, C 1-1-c.
3. Stanley Mallach, "Gothic Furniture Designs by Alexander Jackson Davis," 122–123.

16 Drawing (detail)

Alexander Jackson Davis (1803–1892)
New York, New York, ca. 1841–1847
Pencil on paper
H. 9⅓ (23.5) W. 5⅞ (15)
Avery Architectural Library, Columbia University, New York, New York, A. J. Davis Collection   C 1-1-m

17 Armchair

Probably designed by Alexander Jackson Davis (1803–1892)
New York, New York, ca. 1866
Oak
H. 55 (139.70) W. 22 (55.88) D. 19 (48.26)
Lyndhurst, National Trust for Historic Preservation, Tarrytown, New York
NT 64.25.685 a

Although there is no documentation that Alexander Jackson Davis designed this armchair and its mate for Lyndhurst's dining room, all evidence seems to point in this direction. Similar legs, crockets, methods of construction, and use within the room for which they were originally intended tie this chair to other Davis-designed dining chairs in the same room (no. 15). The incised motif running along the rails, similar to Charles Eastlake's designs of the 1870s, implies that the design may have been executed, or at least updated, during the 1860s when Davis was remodeling Lyndhurst for George Merritt.   KSH

18 Child's Side Chair

Gilbert D. Whitmore (active ca. 1843–1865)
Boston, Massachusetts, 1843–1847
Walnut, pine
H. 30¾ (78.11) W. 13½ (34.29) D. 14 (35.56)
Mr. Lee B. Anderson

Gilbert D. Whitmore's label states that he is the "MANUFACTURER OF FASHIONABLE FURNITURE IN ANCIENT & MODERN STYLE." This small chair, probably made for a child, qualifies under both stylistic descriptions. A label precariously pasted on webbing beneath the seat documents the chair as one of the few identifiable Boston examples. According to city directories, Whitmore conducted his business from 346 Washington Street between 1843 and 1847.   DBW

19 Side Chair

Probably New York or New England, ca. 1846
White pine, yellow pine, soft maple
H. 50⅞ (129.31) W. 24 (125.76) D. 22¾ (57.79)
National Museum of History and Technology, Smithsonian Institution, Washington, D.C.
278,110

Because Alexander Jackson Davis designed the Harral-Wheeler House in Bridgeport, Connecticut (no. 185), it is tempting to attribute the designs for the furniture inside it to him as well. Unfortunately, it is impossible to do so. No references exist in either Davis's correspondence or in his journals relating him to the movable contents of the house. The chair does, however, relate to one in Loudon's *Encyclopædia* (figure 2016). Loudon wrote that "It may be executed in easily carved wood, and afterwards painted and gilt so as to imitate oak, ebony, ivory, and gold. This was not an uncommon practice in the more magnificent articles of furniture of former times . . . ."[1]

Penciled on the inside back upholstery rail is the notation "Oak to match bedstead." The inscription probably refers to the chair's original color, oak graining, and not to the walnut graining that was painted over it at a later date. KSH

1. Stanley Mallach, "Gothic Furniture Designs by Alexander Jackson Davis," 120–124. John Claudius Loudon, *An Encyclopædia of Cottage, Farm, and Villa Architecture and Furniture*, 1094–1095.

20 Side Chair
Attributed to Thomas Brooks (1811–1887)
Brooklyn, New York, ca. 1846
Black walnut, black cherry
H. 40¾ (103.51) W. 17¼ (43.97) D. 17⅛ (43.51)
Society for the Preservation of New England Antiquities, Boston, Massachusetts
1970.436A

21 Armchair
Attributed to Thomas Brooks (1811–1887)
Brooklyn, New York, ca. 1846
Black walnut, black cherry
H. 49 (124.46) W. 20⅞ (53.11) D. 20 (50.80)
Society for the Preservation of New England Antiquities, Boston, Massachusetts
1970.427

When Henry Chandler Bowen (1813–1896) engaged Joseph C. Wells to build a "pointed style" cottage for him in Woodstock, Connecticut, he decided to furnish it in the same mode (see no. 187).[1] Fortunately, both Henry Bowen's expense ledger and Roseland's original contents remained with the house. Noteworthy entries in the ledger for Bowen's "Dwelling House &c[,] Woodstock Conn" include:

Nov 28 [, 1846]	Cash Insurance on furniture	$ 8[.]50
Dec 19	Cash for Chairs. (J Bradley)	45
22	Cash for Housepaper (English)	32[.]76
Feb 5 [, 1847]	Paid freight of furniture	37[.]32
Feb 13	Mr Brooks bill of furniture	1085[.]21
March 2	Mr Sloans bill carpeting	474[.]79
June 10	Paid Freight on furniture	10[.]50[2]

It seems likely that the bulk of Roseland's furniture was made by Thomas Brooks, if only because of the great volume ordered from him. The J. Bradley mentioned may be Joseph Bradley, a chairmaker active in New York between 1835 and 1860.

The two chairs pictured here are presumably by Brooks. With boldly pierced backs and crisp quatrefoils within ogee arches, the chairs are much

18

18a

20

19

21

19

22

24

23

25

more sophisticated than others of the period (no. 31). Acorn finials cap their rectangular posts, a milk thistle tops each arch, and tapered front legs bring the chairs to visually fragile resting points. Unfortunately Brooks has rather unsuccessfully adapted Restauration-style arms to the armchair. KSH

1. Ruth Davidson, "Roseland, a Gothic Revival Mansion," *Antiques* LXXXI (May 1962), 510–514.
2. Henry C. Bowen, "The Ledger of Henry C. Bowen," 14–15.

22 Side Chair

    Attributed to Thomas Brooks (1811–1887)
    Brooklyn, New York, ca. 1846
    Black walnut, black cherry
    H. 53 (134.62) W. 20 (50.80) D. 19¼ (48.90)
    Society for the Preservation of New England Antiquities, Boston, Massachusetts
    1970.426

Nineteenth-century design books frequently refer to the "correctness" or "suitability" of Gothic Revival furnishings for drawing rooms and libraries, but they seldom comment on revivalist chairs in terms of comfort. Their generally low seats and pierced, unupholstered, upright backs make them anything but comfortable for casual sitting. This chair, part of the larger set at Roseland attributed to Thomas Brooks, tries to resolve the problem: two trefoil arches rise from a square upholstered back. The result is a more comfortable, but certainly more disjointed, design with wild arches and crockets tacked on to an austere, rectangular seat and back. KSH

23 Armchair

    Design attributed to James Renwick, Jr. (1818–1895)
    Washington, D.C., 1846–1855
    Walnut
    H. 55 (139.70) W. 26 (66.04) D. 23½ (59.69)
    On loan from the Smithsonian Institution Furnishings Collection, Washington, D.C.
    SI 71.18

James Renwick, Jr., was one of twelve men who competed to design the original Smithsonian Institution building. The four surviving proposals, including Renwick's, were all in the Gothic or Roman styles.[1] Renwick's final plans specified the "FINISH OF REGENTS' ROOM AND BAY WINDOW CONNECTED WITH IT" as: "Eighteen heavily carved arm Chairs, and one heavily carved table in the Norman style, will be carved for the Regents' room, from best black walnut, varnished 4 coats and polished. The whole to be carved according to the designs and directions of the Architect."[2]

At least nine chairs survive from this group in six similar but not identical patterns. All have high, flat, upholstered backs, galleried arms, and aggressive use of architectural elements. The chair pictured here, which is one of a pair, has a steeply pitched crest rail and vertical drops (vergeboards, as Downing called them) that form a decorative combination seen in many modest pointed cottages, among them Glenn Cottage in Roxbury, Massachusetts.[3]   KSH

1. James M. Goode, "The Smithsonian Institution Building," 3-4.
2. "Specifications of the Carpenters' and Joiners' Work for the Smithsonian Institution, Timber," from the files of the Smithsonian Institution, Washington, D.C., 6.
3. Andrew Jackson Downing, *The Architecture of Country Houses*, 105; and William Bailey Lang, *Views, with Ground Plans, of the Highland Cottages at Roxbury*, n. p.

24 Armchair
    Design attributed to James Renwick, Jr. (1818–1895)
    Washington, D.C., 1846–1855
    Walnut
    H. 55 (139.70) W. 26 (66.04) D. 23½ (59.69)
    On loan from the Smithsonian Institution Furnishings Collection, Washington, D.C.
    SI 66.87

This chair clearly owes its design to those remarkable late Gothic rose windows seen in such cathedrals as Rheims and Lincoln. Chairs of this type are more like thrones than like armchairs—perhaps James Renwick's subtle comment on the functionaries who used them. The thronelike impression is hardly relieved by the gilding that highlights these examples. With a roughly finished back, the chair was designed to stand against a wall.   KSH

25 Side Chair
    United States, ca. 1840–1860
    Mahogany
    H. 37½ (85.25) W. 17 (43.08) D. 15 (38.00)
    Mr. Lee B. Anderson

Although rather small in scale, this chair exhibits extraordinarily high quality both in design and craftsmanship. Twisted columns have been subtly combined with arches, crockets, and finials to create an image far more Gothic than the individual motif would otherwise suggest. The carved detail of the rail and crest is especially fine. Use of mahogany in pure Gothic designs is far less common than use of walnut or even oak.   DBW

26 Armchair
    Possibly John and Joseph W. Meeks (active partnership 1836–1860)
    New York, New York, ca. 1836–1857
    Walnut
    H. 53 (134.62) W. 23 (58.42) D. 22 (55.88)
    Mr. Lee B. Anderson

The back of this large armchair with its complicated tracery recalls the façade of a Gothic cathedral, and the rose window motif in the upper central area strengthens that image. The spiral turnings of the stiles, arm supports, and front legs, while not unusual, are seen less often than the bobbin-turned treatment of the armchair (no. 27). Particularly unusual, however, are the molded, curving arms. This chair is closely related to an example made by John and Joseph W. Meeks now in a Providence, Rhode Island, collection. While this chair is made of walnut, a similar model made of oak also is known.   DBW

27 Armchair
    United States, ca. 1840–1860
    Walnut
    H. 49⅛ (124.75) W. 22¼ (56.50) D. 20¾ (52.70)
    Colorado Springs Fine Arts Center, Colorado Springs, Colorado; Debutante Ball Committee Purchase Funds   1972.129

Tracery back, bobbin-turned stiles, partly upholstered arms with ball terminals, and elongated urn finials join in a combination occasionally seen in the

26

27

28

29

Gothic period. This chair's present owner suggests that it may have been made in New York. Although that provenance is also suggested for a similar child's armchair (no. 28), no labeled piece in this style has surfaced to help document either example. This chair was originally owned by Mr. and Mrs. John M. Huiskamp, who immigrated to St. Louis, Missouri, from Holland in 1847.   KSH

28 Child's Armchair

United States, ca. 1840–1860
Walnut, pine
H. 32 (81.28) W. 14½ (36.83) D. 13½ (34.29)
Mr. Frank Brozyna

Despite its small size, the attention to detail and the quality of craftsmanship make this child's armchair equal in every respect to comparable full-sized chairs (no. 29). The design elements—window-like back flanked by columns contained within turned stiles—relate this chair to the large armchair above (no. 27) that probably is from New York, suggesting a similar provenance here.   DBW

29 Side Chair

United States, ca. 1840–1860
Walnut
H. 38 (96.52) W. 17½ (44.33) D. 17 (43.18)
Lyman Allyn Museum, New London, Connecticut   1936.3.156

The relationship between this side chair and the bobbin-turned child's armchair (no. 28) is immediately obvious. They share virtually the same back. Full-sized armchairs with similar backs are also known. Chairs like these show that by altering parts, the nineteenth-century cabinetmaker achieved a degree of versatility that greatly expanded his normal product line.   KSH

30 Side Chair

Possibly Daniels and Hitchins (active partnership ca. 1850–1868)
Troy, New York, 1856
Mahogany
H. 55¼ (140.34) W. 20¼ (51.44) D. 19 (48.26)
The Brooklyn Museum, Brooklyn, New York, Dick S. Ramsay Fund   40.554

"Looking Glasses, Furniture of all descriptions, Hair Seating, Curled Hair, Upholster's [sic] Trimmings, Feathers and Feather Beds, Mahogany, Veneer, and all articles in their line of business kept constantly on hand," advertised Albe C. Daniels and John Hitchins in the first year of their partnership.[1] Five years later they sold this simple but sophisticated chair to Colonel Robert J. Milligan of Saratoga Springs.[2] The chair reflects a slender sense of proportion and a good bit of hand work. Its incised work is carved, usually on two planes, rather than being cut and applied; its crockets are flowing and crisp; and even the points on its center quatrefoil terminate in berry-like trefoils. The three-part milk thistle capping the chair completes a design that in almost every instance uses elements in multiples of threes and fours.   KSH

1. John F. Prescott, *John F. Prescott's City and Business Directory for 1850–1* (Troy, New York: John F. Prescott, 1850), n.p.
2. The chair was purchased by the present owners from Miss Sarah F. Milligan, daughter of the original owner. The bill of sale still with the chair confirms that it was purchased on June 27, 1856, by Colonel Robert J. Milligan of 102 Circular Street, Saratoga Springs, New York.

31 Side Chair

United States, ca. 1850–1860
Walnut
H. 46¾ (118.75) W. 18⅛ (46.1) D. 17⅛ (43.5)
Mrs. Charles H. Lewis, Jr.

Made with minimal hand work and maximum use of a bandsaw, this chair is an efficient product of an industrial age. The splat has been pierced by a saw, and its edges have not been planed. The stiles are actually two machine-cut parallel pieces of wood glued together and covered by a ¹⁄₁₆-inch veneer that has also been pierced by saw. After the basic frame was assembled, machine-cut veneers were added to its surface across its front seat rail and splat. As final touches, casters were inserted into its front legs, and three independently crafted crockets were joined to its back. There is another virtually identical chair in a Washington, D.C., collection.

Family tradition states that the Lewis chair belonged to Amos Lum (1792–1862) of Newark, New Jersey, or to his daughter Hannah (Mrs. Charles Freeman, b. 1825 in Newark, d. 1889 in Macon, Georgia) or to her brother Samuel Y. Lum. It has descended directly through the Freemans to the present owner, who brought it to Texas from Georgia.   KSH

32 Side Chair
    Probably United States, ca. 1840–1860
    Rosewood
    H. 46¾ (118.80) W. 19⅝ (49.80) D. 18¼ (46.30)
    Museum of Fine Arts, Boston, Massachusetts,
        Gift of Mr. and Mrs. Richard C. Hill
        Res. 65.75

"Alert" aptly describes this modest side chair. Its milk thistle crockets and finials stand upright, further accenting the vertical feeling desirable in pure Gothic furniture. For many years the chair stood in a house on Creston Avenue in Fordham, New York.
    KSH

33 Child's Armchair
    United States, ca. 1850–1860
    Walnut
    H. 30¼ (76.84) W. 14½ (36.83) D. 13½ (34.29)
    National Park Service, Longfellow National
        Historic Site, Cambridge, Massachusetts
        Catalogue No. 382

Distinctively turned stiles are the most conspicuous decorations on this diminutive armchair. The heavy ball turnings on its front stiles form an obvious contrast to its much more subdued rear rails and unencumbered back, all of which are capped by rather attenuated urn finials. This is not the only Gothic Revival chair to use urns as a decorative device; another child's armchair (no. 28) uses them as well. According to tradition, this armchair belonged to the children of poet Henry Wadsworth Longfellow.   KSH

30

32

31

33

34a

34

36

35

37

34 Side Chair*

George J. Henkels (active 1843–1877)[1]
Philadelphia, Pennsylvania, ca. 1853–1857
Walnut
H. 40 (101.60) W. 15 (38.10) D. 16 (40.64)
Mr. Lee B. Anderson

A solid wood back with upholstered panel is extremely unusual. The remaining members, legs and stiles, are bobbin-turned in the Elizabethan manner, and placement of the Gothic back, simply supported between the sides, suggests that interchangeable parts in either the Elizabethan or Gothic styles could have been used to create whichever mode was desired. The chair bears fragments of a label reading "GEORGE J HENKELS." The label is set in the same type face as a Henkels sales brochure published between 1853 and 1857 in which he advertised Gothic hall chairs in oak, walnut, or mahogany for nine or twelve dollars.[2]   DBW

1. Kenneth Ames, "George Henkels, Nineteenth-Century Cabinetmaker," *Antiques* CIV (October 1973), 641–650.
2. *George J. Henkels. City Cabinet Warerooms, 173 Chestnut St. Philadelphia*, [Philadelphia, ca. 1853], 15.

35 Doll's Chair

United States, ca. 1840–1860
Mahogany
H. 28½ (72.39) W. 10½ (26.67) D. 12 (30.48)
Mr. Lee B. Anderson

Frequently the borderline between the Elizabethan and Gothic styles was very thin. In this small example the strapwork elements of the back are very much in the Elizabethan taste, but the Gothic trefoils and central ogee arch predominate.   DBW

36 Side Chair

Possibly Alexander Roux (active ca. 1837–1881)
New York, New York, ca. 1852
H. 40 (101.60) W. 18 (45.72) D. 18 (45.72)
Mr. Lee B. Anderson

This chair is both well-proportioned and of less complex design than many other Gothic Revival chairs. It relies almost exclusively on cusped arches to shape its back in a utilitarian and restful form. The chair is seemingly identical to a set of chairs in a private collection in Geneva, New York, which survive with their original bill of sale documenting their purchase from Alexander Roux's firm in 1852. This chair was formerly used at Tioranda, a brick villa in Dutchess County, New York. KSH

37 Armchair

Possibly Massachusetts, ca. 1855–1865
Black walnut
H. 48 (121.92) W. 25 (63.50) D. 23 (58.42)
Essex Institute, Salem, Massachusetts
121, 719

Timid crockets, a low crest rail confused by a screen of imaginative but unarchitectural arches, and arms merging into stiles, all point to an unadorned design from the third quarter of the nineteenth century that uses Gothic material but is not dominated by it. The seat, back, and arms of the chair are embroidered with Berlin work, and the piece bears a hand-written label under the seat: "Worked by Caroline E. Smith, Boston, about 1861." Nothing more is known about Caroline Smith. KSH

38 Side Chair

John Jelliff (1813–1893)
Newark, New Jersey, ca. 1855
Rosewood
H. 58¾ (149.33) W. 18 (45.72)
Collection of the Newark Museum, Newark, New Jersey
54.13

In overall design few Gothic Revival side chairs are as successful as this John Jelliff example. With its undulating upholstered back, pierced quatrefoil, and finely crocketed crest rail, it is a truly appealing piece. Even more exceptional is the fact that the chair is documented. It was designed and made by her father for Mary C. P. Peshine (nee Jelliff, born 1841, daughter of John and Mary Marsh Jelliff). Mary Peshine's daughter Florence Peshine Eagleton (Mrs. Wells P. Eagleton) inherited the chair and subsequently bequeathed it to its present owner in 1954.[1]

John Jelliff was born in Norwalk, Connecticut, and apprenticed under Lemuel M. and Daniel B. Crane of Newark until 1835. After ending a partnership with Thomas L. Vantilburg (1836–1843), he operated his own shop at 301–303 Broad Street (1843–1860), first with Henry H. Miller as an apprentice and then with Miller as a partner. Jelliff retired in 1860, but Miller continued to operate John Jelliff and Company until his own retirement in 1890.[2]

KSH

1. The Newark Museum also owns approximately 150 of Jelliff's drawings of furniture in several different styles. On one, a miscellaneous assortment of Gothic table tops and chair backs, he scribbled, "A. W. N. Pugin on Gothic Furniture," indicating at least passing familiarity with the Englishman's designs. See also, *19th-Century America: Furniture and Other Decorative Arts*, no. 104.
2. J. Stewart Johnson, "John Jelliff, Cabinetmaker," *Antiques* CII (August 1972), 256–261.

39 Side Chair

John Jelliff (1813–1893)
Newark, New Jersey, ca. 1845–1860
Mahogany
H. 35 (88.90) W. 19 (48.16) D. 22 (55.88)
Mr. Lee B. Anderson

In this example, John Jelliff has applied two Gothic motifs, the trefoil and quatrefoil, to a basically Rococo Revival form. Compact proportions, vigorous carved detail, and short, stubby cabriole legs relate to extant Jelliff drawings. Yet Jelliff's interpretation here is far less specifically Gothic than it is in another known example (no. 38). The use of rich heavy upholstery, both in the seat and in the back, conforms to fashions introduced at the middle of the nineteenth century. The chair was purchased by its present owner from one of John Jelliff's great-granddaughters. DBW

38

39

40

41

42

40   Side Chair
Probably United States, ca. 1850
Walnut
H. 41½ (105.41) W. 18¾ (47.63) D. 18½ (46.99)
Collections of Greenfield Village and the Henry Ford Museum, Dearborn, Michigan
28.899.152

Just as Gothic and Restauration styles were often wedded in a single chair or case piece in the 1830s (see nos. 1 and 7) so, too, were Gothic and Rococo Revival styles combined in the middle of the century. Here the crest rail of rich Rococo Revival design surmounts an austere back that is pierced by a stylized Gothic trefoil arch and softened by interlacing Rococo foliage. The end product is a strange, but nevertheless pleasant, amalgam.[1]   KSH

1. *Art and the Excited Spirit: America in the Romantic Period*, edited by David Carew Huntington, Edward R. Molnar, and Robert A. Yassin, 63.

41   Side Chair
Possibly New York, ca. 1850–1860
Mahogany
H. 33 (83.82) W. 17½ (44.40) D. 18 (45.72)
Mr. Lee B. Anderson

In general outline the back of this side chair retains the flowing curvilinear lines of the Rococo Revival, while at the same time it clearly makes a Gothic statement. The resultant undulating arches are most unusual. While the lower section is basically rectilinear and less bold, the splayed front legs echo the line above and effectively unify the composition. One of a pair formerly in the Hurst-Pierrepont House, the chair predates by several years the Alexander Jackson Davis house built in Garrison, New York, in 1863.   DBW

42   Side Chair
Possibly Thomas Brooks (1811–1887)
Brooklyn, New York, ca. 1850–1860
Walnut
H. 46½ (119.11) W. 20 (50.80) D. 18 (45.72)
Mr. Lee B. Anderson

The finesse with which the Rococo and the Gothic modes are commingled is unusual; the undulating line of the back, echoing eighteenth-century prototypes, enhances the transition between the curvilinear Rococo base and the architectural Gothic back. The chair was owned by a Charleston, South Carolina, family who by tradition ascribed this chair to Thomas Brooks. A seemingly identical chair appears in a photograph of a stair hall in the Robert Kelly house at 9 West 16th Street, New York. The home, designed by Richard Upjohn in the 1840s, was photographed during the third quarter of the nineteenth century.[1]   DBW

1. Interior photographs of the Kelly house are in the collections of the Museum of the City of New York. We are grateful to Carol E. Gordon of the Munson-Williams-Proctor Institute in Utica, New York, for calling our attention to the photographs.

43 Side Chair

United States, ca. 1850–1865
Rosewood
H. 37 (93.98) W. 16 (40.64) D. 15 (38.10)
Mr. Frank Brozyna

Rococo Revival forms blended with and in some cases overwhelmed Gothic ornament as evinced in this side chair, one of four that were once in the same parlor. Heavy cabriole legs, a serpentine seat, and foliated back are obvious Rococo elements in the chair, while the vestigial crockets and mildly arched back with arches and trefoil drops above the seat recall the Gothic. Here is a chair that clearly combines elements from two revivals.   KSH

44 Hall Chair

Possibly Philadelphia, Pennsylvania, ca. 1842
Mahogany, pine
H. 37 (93.98) W. 14½ (36.83) D. 14 (35.56)
Mr. Lee B. Anderson

This unusually small hall chair with solid back and plank seat reflects English prototypes, but the console-shaped front legs and serpentine seat are in the Restauration mode. The chair has a history of ownership in the Philadelphia area. A small paper label reading "Phila. 1842" is affixed to the bottom under the seat. Reports of the Franklin Institute indicate that Gothic furniture was being exhibited there during the early 1840s.[1] Whether or not this example was made in Philadelphia or merely sold there is not clear at this time.   DBW

1. "Report of the Committee on Premieres and Exhibitions of the Franklin Institute," *Journal of the Franklin Institute* (Philadelphia, 1842), 12.

45 Hall Chair

Possibly John and Joseph W. Meeks (active partnership ca. 1836–1859)
New York, New York, ca. 1852
Mahogany
H. 44 (111.76) W. 20½ (52.07) D. 19 (48.26)
Mr. Lee B. Anderson

A most unusual feature of this otherwise fairly straightforward hall chair with modified rose-window back is the use of tapering clustered columns to form the front legs. The architectural overtones of this treatment are strengthened by the flat Tudor arches formed by brackets under the seat rail.

This chair was bought from a descendant of its original owner, who lived in a Long Island house. By tradition all the furnishings in this home were purchased in 1852 from the Meeks family.   DBW

46 Hall Chair

United States, ca. 1840–1850
Rosewood, walnut
H. 43¾ (111.13) W. 18½ (47.00) D. 15½ (39.37)
Anne and David Sellin

In this and another seemingly identical example in a private collection in Tarrytown, New York, the rose window motif has been glamorized and adapted to the back of a hall chair. The lively nipped waist, crockets, top finial, and four swirling quatrefoils cut from one piece of wood make the design a significant departure from its stained glass source and much less academic than Alexander Jackson Davis's wheel-back model (nos. 12 and 188). The front legs, like those of another hall chair (no. 47), are turned and ringed at the ankle much like English chairs of the 1820s and 1830s.[1]   KSH

1. John Claudius Loudon, *An Encyclopædia of Cottage, Farm, and Villa Architecture and Furniture* (1833), reprinted in *Furniture for the Victorian Home*, 112–113.

46

47 Hall Chair

United States, ca. 1840–1855
Black walnut, eastern white pine
H. 51¾ (131.45) W. 17⅝ (44.77) D. 17¾ (45.09)
Private Collection

Hall chairs were not so much for people to sit upon as they were temporary stopping points for visitors passing in and out of a home. Their rigid backs, which meet their seats at right angles, and hard, hinged lids for convenient stashing of gloves and other outdoor apparel in the well below hardly lend themselves to comfortable sitting. However, their bold turnings and high, crocketed backs with pierced splats such as the one seen here helped create a romantic entrance to any nineteenth-century home. This chair was bought at an auction in Morris, New York. Its seat and each seat rail are marked with a Roman "XII." A seemingly identical chair is illustrated in Thomas Ormsbee's *Field Guide*.[1]   KSH

1. Thomas H. Ormsbee, *Field Guide to American Victorian Furniture*, 65–66.

47

48 Hall Chair

United States, ca. 1851–1856
Oak
H. 68 (172.70) W. 21½ (54.60) D. 10½ (26.60)
The Estate of Mrs. Hubert F. Barnum, Natchez, Mississippi

During the last great flowering of antebellum Natchez, Frederick Stanton of Belfast, Ireland, built Stanton Hall near the center of the town for his young wife, Hulda Helm.[1] Stanton placed four remarkable hall chairs in the Gothic taste in the hall of his otherwise Greek Revival home. Although treatment of the seat rail on this chair is similar to seat-rail treatment of at least two other chairs (nos. 21 and 30), this is the only hall chair with pierced stiles. It joins other hall chairs in having a glove well, ogee back legs, and an upright back, but far surpasses most examples in its undulating fluidity of design that is truly reminiscent of Europe's original High Gothic. Trefoil arches like those at the base of the back must have originally formed a skirt below the seat.   KSH

1. Nola Nance Oliver, *Natchez, Symbol of the Old South* (New York: Hastings House Publishers, 1940), 96–97; and Celia Jackson Otto, *American Furniture of the Nineteenth Century*, 118.

49 Easy Chair

Probably United States, ca. 1852
Walnut
H. 43⅝ (110.69)
Lent by The Metropolitan Museum of Art, New York, New York, Rogers Fund, 1967
67.148

Deep-seated easy chairs are welcome reliefs when compared with many less comfortable side and hall chairs in the Gothic Revival style. Surprisingly, they appear to be rather rare, although similar tufted, upholstered examples with exposed wood posts were frequently seen in the classical style.[1] This chair descended in the Delano family of Barrytown, New York, and was probably among the original furnishings of their 1852 home, Steen Valetje.[2] Its restful form, pointed stiles, quatrefoils, and double-ended horseshoe arches made it an appropriate addition to the Gothic library there. The motifs on its legs and seat rail are very closely allied to those of the Daniels and Hitchins side chair (no. 30). KSH

1. John Claudius Loudon, *An Encyclopædia of Cottage, Farm, and Villa Architecture and Furniture*, nos. 1925, 1926.
2. *19th-Century America: Furniture and Other Decorative Arts*, no. 102.

50 Piano Stool
    Probably New York, New York, ca. 1835–1845
    Mahogany veneer on pine
    H. 34½ (87.63) W. 12 (30.48) D. 11½ (29.21)
    Mr. Lee B. Anderson

Severe lines and plain surfaces of the Restauration style have been embellished with Gothic detail, resulting in a pleasingly architectural composition of the arcade, trefoil frieze, and trefoil design. The quality of craftsmanship is extremely high, suggesting manufacture either by the Meeks family or by another leading New York maker. Oral tradition states that this stool is one of a number of Gothic pieces once owned by the Gracie family of New York. DBW

51 Child's Rocking Chair
    Frost, Peterson and Company
    New York, New York, ca. 1868–1880
    Walnut, "perforated veneer"
    H. 25½ (64.75) W. 14 (35.55) D. 21 (53.3)
    Harris County Heritage Society, Houston, Texas

This little rocker illustrates a style in decline; there is no romantic connotation or medieval feeling. The two arches punched in the back of its molded seat bear no relationship to the flower-painted crest rail and arms, to the star punched in the seat, or to the design as a whole. Pressed into the top of the seat is the following inscription: "FROST PETERSON & CO. / N.Y. / FROST MANU'S PATENT / Dec. 20, 1865 / [N]O[V] 18, 1868." Interestingly, Gardner and Company of New York in conjunction with the Philadelphia Centennial advertised similar chairs with "Perforated Veneer Seats."[1] KSH

1. See James D. McCabe, *The Illustrated History of the Centennial Exhibition*, 754; and Kenneth Leroy Ames, "Renaissance Revival Furniture in America," 485, 496–497.

48

50

49

51

52 Hall Bench

Philadelphia, Pennsylvania, ca. 1840–1850
Oak, tulipwood
H. 15½ (39.37) W. 22 (55.88) D. 78 (198.12)
Mr. and Mrs. James Biddle

Made for the hall of the 1840s Gothic cottage at Andalusia, this bench is en suite with an armchair (no. 9). The low, narrow, rectangular form both eminently suits its designated location and also avoids the problems of overly elaborate Gothic design discussed by Andrew Jackson Downing when considering hall furniture.[1]

DBW

1. Andrew Jackson Downing, *The Architecture of Country Houses*, p. 440.

53 Window Seat

Attributed to Thomas Brooks (1811–1887)
Brooklyn, New York, ca. 1846
Black walnut, black cherry
H. 24¼ (61.60) W. 92½ (234.95) D. 20 (50.80)
Society for the Preservation of New England Antiquities, Boston, Massachusetts
1970.429

On July 23, 1847, Henry C. Bowen paid $132.52 for the stained glass in Roseland (no. 186).[1] It was appropriate, therefore, that he should ask Thomas Brooks to make a window seat to fit within the bay of one of these stained-glass windows, a feature directly associated with Gothic cathedrals. Although there certainly were no medieval prototypes for window seats and the seat by necessity had to be long and low rather than tall and pointed, Brooks has carefully picked up the quatrefoils and vines on the legs and rails of other pieces in the set and combined them with a low upholstered back rail supported by a gallery of chubby trefoil arches. The overall effect is pleasing, if not very archeological.

KSH

1. Henry C. Bowen, "The Ledger of Henry C. Bowen," 15.

54 Couch*

Possibly by John and Joseph W. Meeks (active partnership, ca. 1836–1860)
New York, New York, ca. 1840–1855
Mahogany, oak, pine
H. 41 (104.14) W. 78 (198.12) D. 30 (76.20)
Mr. Lee B. Anderson

This couch, open at one end, continues the concept of the French or Grecian sofa introduced at the turn of the nineteenth century. Here the form has been updated with the introduction of rich tufted upholstery, a mid-nineteenth-century innovation; it is ornamented with fashionable Gothic and Elizabethan detail. The molded and ogee-arched skirt relates to the treatment of a gaming table (no. 77) that has Meeks associations, and it may be that this example is also from that group. By tradition this couch was owned by the Gracie family in New York.

DBW

54

55 Couch

Probably New York or New England, ca. 1846
Yellow poplar, white pine, paint
H. 55 (139.70) W. 75¼ (190.14) D. 35 (88.90)
National Museum of History and Technology, Smithsonian Institution, Washington, D.C.
278,110

Gothic Revival couches are probably more closely derived from classical and exotic modes à la Madame Récamier than from eighteenth-century daybeds. This remarkable couch, which is from the same set as a side chair (no. 19), was made for the Harral-Wheeler House. What the couch lacks in beauty it makes up for in cleverness of design. Perhaps most conspicuous are its column, block, and bun legs originally painted with an oak graining; at a later date maple and walnut graining was applied to the oak base.

KSH

55

56

56 Settee
>Attributed to Thomas Brooks (1811–1887)
>Brooklyn, New York, ca. 1846
>Black walnut, black cherry.
>H. 60⅝ (154.05) W. 81 (225.74) D. 23½ (59.69)
>Society for the Preservation of New England Antiquities, Boston, Massachusetts
>1970.438

57 Settee
>Attributed to Thomas Brooks (1811–1887)
>Brooklyn, New York, ca. 1846
>Black walnut, black cherry
>H. 52⅝ (133.73) W. 61⅞ (157.24)
>D. 22¾ (57.94)
>Society for the Preservation of New England Antiquities, Boston, Massachusetts
>1970.428

Like other seats at Henry Bowen's Roseland (no. 22), the settees rely on Gothic elements rising from solid, upholstered backs. The smaller settee conforms to mid-nineteenth-century taste for using chairbacks in multiples. The larger settee retains the same angularity as the smaller but emphasizes a larger center section, which contributes mass as well as size to the piece. Both settees lend credence to Brooks's advertisement for "ROSEWOOD & MAHOGANY / CABINET FURNITURE / on an extensive scale, of entirely new and beautiful patterns, which will defy all competition either in this city or New York, as regards taste, workmanship, durability or cheapness. ... All or any kind of cabinet furniture and chairs made to order, and warranted."[1]   KSH

1. *Brooklyn Directory and Yearly Advertiser for 1846 & 7* (Brooklyn: William J. Hearne, and Edwin Van Nostrand, n.d.), n.p.

58 Footstool
>Attributed to Thomas Brooks (1811–1887)
>Brooklyn, New York, ca. 1846
>Mahogany, mahogany veneer, pine
>H. 16 (40.64) W. 22½ (57.15) D. 20½ (50.07)
>Society for the Preservation of New England Antiquities, Boston, Massachusetts
>1970.434A

This low footstool is part of the same set made for Henry C. Bowen's Roseland as the window seat

57

58

(no. 53). Like the window seat it derives its Gothic feeling not from arches but from quatrefoils on its rails and tapering, hexagonal legs. While the footstool is only attributed to Thomas Brooks (see no. 21), it is interesting to note that Brooks's name appears on a Bowen family guest list in the late 1860s. Evidently Bowen and Brooks remained friends although they did not continue their business relationship. In 1853 Bowen bought a large house in Brooklyn, which he furnished in Rococo and Renaissance Revival styles from the shop of John Henry Belter.[1]   KSH

1. The information on Henry C. Bowen has been supplied through the courtesy of Richard C. Nylander, Curator of Collections, Society for the Preservation of New England Antiquities, Boston, Massachusetts.

59a

59

59 Garden Bench
John Timmes
Brooklyn, New York, ca. 1878–1895
Cast iron
H. 38½ (97.79) W. 46½ (118.11) D. 19½ (49.53)
David Allen Hanks, Philadelphia, Pennsylvania

According to Brooklyn city directories in the 1850s, Peter Timmes (or Timms) was a nailmaker working in the city. Evidently his son John learned the craft and continued under his father's name with at least two ventures into cast-iron furniture. In the 1878–1879 city directory John Timmes appeared as a spikemaker, and his company, Peter Timmes Son, received its first listing. The bench was made between 1878 and the mid-1890s, when the company ceased to be listed. The name of the firm, "PETER TIMMES SON BROOKLYN N. Y. / PAT. APP D FOR," is cast on its back center section.

Unlike those made at the height of the Gothic Revival between 1830 and 1870, this bench in no way implies any relationship between it and an earlier medieval form. Instead, Timmes has applied a pierced skirt terminating in trefoils to a basically Eastlake form.[1] He also applied classical ornamentation to a similar iron bench at approximately the same time.[2] In both instances the romantic feeling for the exotic, so apparent in midcentury America, has been

60

supplanted by a new movement with vestigial remains from the old. KSH

1. *Eastlake-Influenced American Furniture, 1870–1890*, no. 56.
2. *19th-Century America: Furniture and Other Decorative Arts*, no. 237.

60 Bench*

Probably New York, New York, 1837–1850
Oak, ebony black finish, sugar maple
H. 52 (132.08) W. 52 (132.08) D. 25 (63.50)
Mr. Lee B. Anderson

In discussing furniture suitable for the hall, Andrew Jackson Downing illustrates a highly architectural bench in the round-arched Romanesque or Norman style and relates that this furniture is usually too clumsy for drawing rooms or parlors.[1] This hall bench of extraordinarily high quality is quite architectural and was, according to oral history, made for Samuel E. Lyon's Gothic cottage in White Plains, New York, a home designed by Alexander Jackson Davis. DBW

1. Andrew Jackson Downing, *The Architecture of Country Houses*, 460.

61 Sofa Table

Probably United States, ca. 1840
Mahogany, mahogany veneer
H. 30¼ (76.84) W. 42¾ (108.59) D. 27 5/16 (69.37)
On loan from the Smithsonian Institution Furnishings Collection, Washington, D.C.

"*Sofa-tables*, are elegant small tables for the drawing room, of a convenient form, as their name implies, to be placed near the sofa, and, for this purpose, are long and narrow. They are always made of fine woods, and considerably enriched by carving, inlaying, or other modes of ornamenting."[1] This conservative table with carefully matched veneers would not be part of the Gothic Revival were it not for the graceful arch and austere drop stabilizing its legs. The ogee arch used in lieu of more common stretchers is not only unusual in concept but also provides stability without impeding foot space below. KSH

1. Thomas Webster and Mrs. [William] Parkes, *An Encyclopædia of Domestic Economy*, 261–262.

62 Pier Table

John Needles (1786–1878)
Baltimore, Maryland, ca. 1835–1853
Mahogany veneer on pine, marble
H. 29½ (74.93) W. 39½ (100.33) D. 19 (48.26)
Mr. Lee B. Anderson

This Gothicized Restauration-style pier table bears the label of John Needles of Baltimore. Needles, a Quaker cabinetmaker, worked in Baltimore from 1808 until his retirement in 1853.[1] This table was owned by the Daingerfield family of Baltimore. DBW

1. A Gothic sofa table, which was presented to Needles's daughter in 1857 and descended in her family, is in the Baltimore Museum of Art (Helen Comstock, *American Furniture: Seventeenth, Eighteenth, and Nineteenth Century Styles*, no. 610). For further information on Needles, see Charles F. Montgomery, "John Needles—Baltimore Cabinetmaker," *Antiques* LXV (April 1954), 292–295.

63 Sofa Table

Possibly Baltimore, Maryland, ca. 1830–1840
Mahogany, mahogany veneer, pine, poplar
H. 28½ (72.4) W. 43 (109.25) D. 23 (58.40)
Anne and David Sellin

Not only does this table have a similar drawer arrangement to a labeled Baltimore piece by John Needles (active 1808–1853),[1] but it also has an interesting and somewhat convoluted history. Penciled underneath the top, which appears to be a replacement, is the word "Bonaparte" or "Buonaparte" in a Victorian script. The table descended in the family of Elizabeth Patterson of Baltimore, who married Jerome Napoleon Bonaparte. In the 1920s the table passed from the Patterson family into the hands of an employee, then to the employee's daughter, and finally to the parents of the present owner. No matter who the original owner, the table's handsome use of mahogany veneers and the softening quality of its cusped arches, which relieve an otherwise angular design, make this piece a fine example.   KSH

1. Charles F. Montgomery, "John Needles—Baltimore Cabinetmaker," *Antiques* LXV (April 1954), 292–295.

64 Pier Table

Joseph Meeks and Sons (active partnership ca. 1829–1835)
New York, New York, ca. 1829–1835
Mahogany, mahogany veneer, marble
H. 36 (91.4) W. 43 (109.2) D. 20 (50.8)
Mr. Graham Williford, Fairfield, Texas

The quality of detail in this pier table is immediately apparent. Fine mahogany veneers, an apron ornamented with tiny turned drops, colonettes at each leg, and a lively lower shelf all mark it and its mate[1] as objects of note in the Gothic style. Not until the marble top is removed does a paper label appear identifying the table as the product of one of New York's better firms, Joseph Meeks and Sons.[2]   KSH

1. The mate to this table is owned by Mr. Lee B. Anderson.
2. An untorn version of this label is reproduced in John N. Pearce, Lorraine W. Pearce, and Robert C. Smith, "The Meeks Family of Cabinetmakers," *Antiques* LXXXV (April 1964), 416, fig. 6.

63

65 Dressing Table
United States, ca. 1835–1845
Mahogany
H. 28 (71.12) W. 31 (78.74) D. 20 (50.80)
Mr. Lee B. Anderson

This simple two-drawer table with turned legs in the late Sheraton style would be of little Gothic interest were it not for the rather well-carved quatrefoils at either side of the drawers. It has a history of ownership in Otsego County, New York, and may have belonged to the Cooper family of Otsego Hall (no. 184).   DBW

66 Pedestal Table
United States, ca. 1850–1860
Walnut, marble
H. 29½ (74.93) DIAM. 13½ (34.29)
Mr. Frank Brozyna

After the middle of the nineteenth century the formal arrangement of parlor sets began to give way to less rigid, more picturesque placement of furniture with the result that more small parlor tables reminiscent of eighteenth-century candlestands began to appear. While the turned stem of this example is not unlike those in the late Sheraton mode, the scrolled legs relate to both the Rococo and Renaissance styles, placing the date of this table after the middle of the century. The ogee Gothic arches and drops of the skirt add a light visual touch. The table has a history of ownership on Staten Island.   DBW

64

64a

65

66

67

67 Pedestal Table

Possibly New York, ca. 1842–1845
Mahogany, mahogany veneer, oak
H. 32 (81.28) DIAM. 54 (137.16)
Munson-Williams-Proctor Institute, Utica, New York, Gift of Mrs. Erving Pruyn
60.171

Round extension tables were rather common in the mid-nineteenth century. The pedestal of this handsome table is decorated with trefoil arches within ogee ones, and the base conveniently stands on four casters.[1] When the table is extended a hexagonal center post emerges from the core of the pedestal to support a center leaf. The table comes from the home of Robert Kelly (1808–1856) of New York, a brownstone built circa 1842–1845 at 9 West 16th Street (see no. 42). According to family tradition, both the home and its furnishings were designed by Richard Upjohn.[2]   KSH

1. Helen Comstock, *American Furniture: Seventeenth, Eighteenth, and Nineteenth Century Styles*, no. 611.
2. Photographs of the house are in the collections of the Museum of the City of New York. The house is discussed in Charles Lockwood, *Bricks and Brownstone: The New York Row House, 1783–1929, An Architectural and Social History* (New York: McGraw-Hill, 1972), 205.

68 Center Table*

Probably New York, 1830–1840
Mahogany, oak, paint
H. 30 (76.20) DIAM. 44 (111.70)
Munson-Williams-Proctor Institute, Utica, New York
58.280

Few tables in the history of the American decorative arts are quite as exotic as this one. A basically classical table with scroll legs and paw feet has been overwhelmed by elaborate japanning hardly equaled since Boston's in the Queen Anne period.[1] An arcade of lancet arches surrounds the pedestal while the top is edged with a skirt of flamboyant arches. The table surface is covered with a potpourri of fanciful Chinese scenes bordered by a band of Chinese characters alternating with classical and Gothic motifs.[2]   KSH

1. Elizabeth Rhoades and Brock Jobe, "Recent Discoveries in Boston Japanned Furniture," *Antiques* CV (May 1974), 1082–1091.
2. Helen Comstock, *American Furniture: Seventeenth, Eighteenth and Nineteenth Century Styles*, nos. 606, 607.

68a

68

69 Dining Table
Possibly designed by Alexander Jackson Davis (1803–1892)
New York, New York, 1841–1866
Oak
H. 30½ (77.47) W. 56¼ (142.88) L. (extended) 138¼ (351.17)
Lyndhurst, National Trust for Historic Preservation, Tarrytown, New York
NT 64.25.686

Two statements about Lyndhurst's hexagonal extension table are certain: it is similar to an earlier published design by Augustus Welby Northmore Pugin, and the papers of Alexander Jackson Davis indicate that he designed tables as well as other furniture for Lyndhurst between 1841 and 1847.[1] Between 1842 and 1844 Davis did design a similar hexagonal table for Samuel E. Lyon's Gothic home in White Plains, New York. The Lyon table is documented by a Davis sketch that he labeled "S.E.L. No. 4 / drawing room / table."

It is tempting to conclude that Davis also designed the Lyndhurst table, but the incised vine on the skirt relates to the Renaissance Revival and Eastlake styles of the 1860s, indicating that if this table was designed in the 1840s it may not have been executed until many years later.   KSH

1. The original drawing of the Lyon table is part of the Davis papers, Avery Architectural Library, Columbia University, New York; see Augustus Welby Northmore Pugin, *Gothic Furniture in the Style of the 15th Century*, pl. 12.

70 Library Table
Design attributed to Alexander Jackson Davis (1803–1892)
New York, New York, ca. 1841–1847
Oak
H. 29¾ (75.57) W. 84½ (214.63) D. 41 (104.14)
Lyndhurst, National Trust for Historic Preservation, Tarrytown, New York
NT 64.25.268

Rudolph Ackermann states that "in the more refined aera [*sic*] of the fourteenth and fifteenth centuries, the materials employed were oak or chestnutwood, carved with great delicacy and taste."[1] His sentiment helps explain why much of Lyndhurst's

Gothic furniture is made of oak. This library table is another example attributed by association to Alexander Jackson Davis. Although no known Davis documentation exists for the table, it is very similar to the A. W. N. Pugin design pictured here.[2] By simplifying Pugin's example, Davis was probably more truthful to genuine medieval furnishings than Pugin was in his most scholarly attempts.   KSH

1. "Fashionable Furniture," in Rudolph Ackermann, ed., *The Repository of Arts, Literature, Fashions, Manufactures, &c*, March 1826, p. 185.
2. Augustus Welby Northmore Pugin, *Gothic Furniture in the Style of the 15th Century*, 13.

71   Pedestal Table

Designed by Alexander Jackson Davis (1803–1892)
New York, New York, 1841
Oak
H. 29¼ (74.30) DIAM. 34½ (87.63)
Lyndhurst, National Trust for Historic Preservation, Tarrytown, New York

NT 64.25.10

Like other furniture at Lyndhurst, this table was designed by Alexander Jackson Davis and is documented as such by a drawing in Davis's hand (no. 188). Its carved leafage is very similar to that in the spandrels of Davis's dining-room chairs (no. 15). In a nice revival-style reusage of medieval motifs, its octagonal base, if inverted, would closely resemble a drop in late medieval English fan vaulting.   KSH

72   Center Table

Possibly New York, ca. 1845–1855
Walnut, pine, marble
H. 29 (73.66) DIAM. 35 (88.90)
Mr. Lee B. Anderson

With its octagonal top, bracketed pedestal, and four-part base, this table relates in overall design to the center table attributed to Thomas Brooks that was made for Henry Bowen Chandler's Roseland in Woodstock, Connecticut (no. 186). However, close comparison, particularly in the treatment of the base, suggests that this example probably came from another New York-area shop. Like a fine Gothic chair (no. 41) the table has a history of Charleston, South Carolina, ownership.   DBW

73   Center Table
   Possibly designed by Alexander Jackson Davis
      (1803–1892)
   New York, New York, ca. 1844
   Walnut, marble
   H. 30 (76.20) DIAM. (at sides) 37 (93.98)
   Mr. Lee B. Anderson

Andrew Jackson Downing pictures various examples of Gothic furniture in *The Architecture of Country Houses*, but few surviving examples can be related to those illustrations. This hexagonal table with cluster columns and tripod base appears to be very similar to one in figure 179, "Drawing Room at Kenwood, Gothic Style," the seat of Joel Rathbone near Albany, New York (no. 187).[1] The table has a history of ownership in the Rathbone family. Although Alexander Jackson Davis did design some Gothic furniture for Rathbone and did make the interior view of Rathbone's house for Downing's *Country Houses*, there is no specific drawing or primary source to prove conclusively that Davis designed this attractive table.[2]   DBW

   1. Andrew Jackson Downing, *The Architecture of Country Houses*, 385.
   2. Davis designed a table for Rathbone in May 1844 (Alexander Jackson Davis, papers, New York Public Library). In September Rathbone wrote him that a cabinetmaker had disappointed him and that he "took the order away from him and I am now adrift again as to a set of Gothic chairs and table" (Alexander Jackson Davis, papers, Avery Architectural Library, Columbia University, New York, II, no. 5–15). Since Rathbone seems to be writing about a dining table and chairs, he may or may not be referring to the center table discussed above.

74

74 Center Table
United States, probably New York, ca. 1840–1860
Walnut, pine
H. 31 (78.74) DIAM. 27 (68.58)
Mr. Lee B. Anderson

In basic form this small table conforms generally to Renaissance Revival design. While far from archeological, it achieves a remarkably architectural effect with the four buttress-like legs and soaring crocketed central arch. The carved detail of the arches and feet is of unusually high quality. Interestingly, the top, which is finished in plain pine, was apparently intended to be covered with fabric. The table was purchased by the present owner from Tioranda, a brick villa in Dutchess County, New York.   DBW

75 Nest of Tables
Possibly New York, New York, ca. 1840–1870
Mahogany
H. 29 (73.66) W. 20½ (52.07) D. 14 (35.56)
Mr. Frank Brozyna

Nesting tables were introduced into English furniture at the end of the eighteenth century. Made in sets of three or four, they were characterized accordingly as trio or quartetto tables. The form appeared in America in the early decades after 1800 and, while never very common, continued to be made throughout the first half of the century. Here the vertical arrangement of Gothic arches is a rather successful adaptation of the style to an extant furniture form.   DBW

75

76 Side Table*

    John and Joseph W. Meeks (active partnership 1836–1860)
    New York, New York, 1836–1847
    Mahogany, marble
    H. 30 (76.20) W. 25½ (64.77) D. 16 (40.64)
    Mr. Lee B. Anderson

Spiral turnings and bandsaw-cut legs relate this side table and its mate very closely to two John and Joseph W. Meeks dressing tables that also have beveled marble tops.[1] While spiral turnings indicate both Elizabethan and Gothic Revival designs, the added touch of an arched border around the table top confirms the Meeks's Gothic intent. This little table is labeled with a stencil reading, "J. & J. W. MEEKS / MAKERS / No. 14 Vesey St. / NEW YORK" (see no. 80a). The Meeks's were established at this address from 1836 to 1847.[2]   KSH

    1. John N. Pearce, Lorraine W. Pearce, and Robert C. Smith, "The Meeks Family of Cabinetmakers," *Antiques* LXXXV (April 1964), 418.
    2. *Ibid.*, 419.

77 Library Game Table*

    United States, possibly New York, ca. 1835–1850
    Mahogany veneer on pine, painted slate
    H. 30 (76.20) W. 43½ (110.49) D. 25 (63.50)
    Mr. Lee B. Anderson

Few tables of any period are quite as exuberant in design as this one. As scroll legs with back-curling feet meet an arched stretcher of equal complexity, urn finials in the base rise toward acorns dropping from a molded skirt pierced with quatrefoils. This Gothic Revival table enjoys all the cluttered earmarks of what twentieth-century observers consider "Victorian." It was obviously made by a skilled professional for someone who could afford the luxury of a table made exclusively for games.   KSH

78

78 Desk

Baltimore, Maryland, 1820–1830
Mahogany, mahogany veneer, satinwood, white pine, poplar
H. 56½ (143.51) W. 54 (137.16) D. 22⅜ (56.85)
Through the courtesy of Peter Hill, United States Antiques, Washington, D.C.

Smooth surfaces and richly figured mahogany veneers of the late Sheraton style, barefooted herm figures reminiscent of ancient civilizations, and repeated arches all combine in this comparatively early venture into the Gothic Revival. The desk and a similar sideboard were probably made in Baltimore, where caryatid case pieces with Gothic Revival elements seem to have been uniquely fashionable.[1] In Baltimore in the 1820s the Gothic taste was not limited to furniture. As early as 1827 Henry D. Gilpin described Charles Harper's house, saying in a letter to his father that John Latrobe had "turned the windows, doors, porches &c. into gothic and given it a beautiful appearance...."[2]   KSH

1. The sideboard is in the collection of the Baltimore Museum of Art. At least three other similar desks remain in Baltimore homes. We are grateful to William Voss Elder III of the Baltimore Museum for kindly sharing his information on this group of furniture.
2. Henry D. Gilpin to Joshua Gilpin, Baltimore, September 6, 1827, as quoted in Ralph D. Gray and Gerald E. Hartdagen, [eds.], "A Glimpse of Baltimore Society in 1827: Letters by Henry D. Gilpin," *Maryland Historical Magazine*, Fall 1974, p. 261.

79 Serving Board

United States, ca. 1837
Walnut, pink marble
H. 35 (88.90) W. 43½ (110.49) D. 18½ (46.99)
Mr. Lee B. Anderson

The ecclesiastic connotations of the Gothic style made it especially appropriate for the furnishing of a rectory or parsonage. This example was presented to Boston Unitarian minister Theodore Parker (1810–1860) by a group of friends in 1837, the year both of his ordination and of his marriage to Lydia Dodge Cabot. Parker later gained prominence in the abolition movement, assisted in the escape of fugitive slaves, and authored "A Letter to the People of the United States Touching the Matter of Slavery" (1848).[1] In design, the Parker table, with its straight legs and large brackets in the form of Gothic tracery between the skirt and legs, makes little reference to the then fashionable Restauration style. Rather the form seems more eighteenth-century in spirit.   DBW

1. *Who Was Who in America: Historical Volume, 1607–1896* (Chicago: Marquis—Who's Who, 1963), 395.

80 Sideboard*

John and Joseph W. Meeks (active partnership ca. 1836–1860)
New York, New York, 1836–1847
Mahogany veneer on pine, maple
H. 51 (129.54) W. 47 (119.38) D. 24 (60.96)
Mr. Lee B. Anderson

Unusually small dimensions make this Restauration-style sideboard a rare example. Inset panels on the china rail and cupboard and the uncommon practice of string inlay introduce Gothic details. While the stylistic details of this sideboard do not readily suggest its maker, happily the name of J. and J. W. Meeks is stenciled on the back of one drawer. This Meeks partnership worked at No. 14 Vesey Street from 1836 to 1847.[1]   DBW

1. John N. Pearce, Lorraine W. Pearce and Robert C. Smith, "The Meeks Family of Cabinetmakers," *Antiques* LXXXV (April 1964), 419.

81

82

83

46

81   Wardrobe

United States, ca. 1825
Mahogany, mahogany veneer
H. 100 (254.00) W. 60 (152.40) D. 24½ (62.23)
Harris County Heritage Society, Houston,
   Texas   62.12

Like other case pieces in this exhibition, this wardrobe combines Classical and Restauration-style austerity with simple Gothic arches, thus blending 1500 years of architectural history. This example by an undetermined maker is very similar to illustration number 28 in the well-known 1833 advertisement of Joseph Meeks and Sons.[1]   KSH

1. For a reproduction of the advertisement, see Helen Comstock, *American Furniture: Seventeenth, Eighteenth, and Nineteenth Century Styles*, 310.

82   Desk and Bookcase

John and Joseph W. Meeks (active partnership 1836–1860)
New York, New York, 1836–1847
Rosewood, satinwood
H. 91¾ (233.05) W. 52⅜ (133.05) D. 23¼ (59.06)
Lent by the Metropolitan Museum of Art, New
   York, New York, Rogers Fund, 1969
                                            69.19 a–h

Simply designed but made of elegant woods subtly enriched with Gothic motifs, this Meeks case piece is composed of decorative elements in multiples of two and four. The bookcase and writing area are lined with fine satinwood. John and Joseph Meeks must have been proud to apply their stencil (no. 80a) on the inside of the slant-front writing surface. A nearly identical labeled J. and J. W. Meeks desk and bookcase is in the collection of the Yale University Art Gallery.[1]   KSH

1. *19th-Century America: Furniture and Other Decorative Arts*, no. 100. John Pearce and Lorraine W. Pearce, "More on the Meeks Cabinetmakers," *Antiques* XC (July 1966), 70.

83   Cabinet and Bookcase

Probably United States, ca. 1835–1840
Mahogany, mahogany veneer, pine
H. 91¼ (231.78) W. 49 (124.46) D. 27⅜ (69.58)
Lent by the Metropolitan Museum of Art, New
   York, New York, Gift of John C. Cattus,
   1967   67.262. 1a–c

This cabinet is obviously the work of a skilled and sophisticated shop. The case is born of that late classical style dependent on careful arrangement of beautifully figured mahogany veneers and smooth concave and convex surfaces. Introducing the Gothic Revival, however, are mullions, two weighty cluster columns in the Gothic style, and a pediment, itself a blend of classical anthemion corners and a flamboyant arched center. With neither label nor documentation, the cabinet's maker is regrettably denied his due.[1]   KSH

1. *19th-Century America: Furniture and Other Decorative Arts*, no. 98.

84   Music Cabinet*

Anthony G. Quervelle (1789–1856)
Philadelphia, Pennsylvania, 1835–1845
Mahogany veneer on pine, marble
H. 38 (96.52) W. 33½ (85.09) D. 18 (45.72)
Mr. Lee B. Anderson

This suave music stand is stamped on the marble top and on the back of the cabinet with the label that Anthony G. Quervelle used from 1835 to 1845.[1] While the overall design of clean, crisp lines reflects the Philadelphia interpretation of the Restauration style, a pair of lancet arches and a central pendant introduce the medieval Gothic to the mirror door.   DBW

1. Robert C. Smith, "The Furniture of Anthony G. Quervelle, Part IV: Some Case Pieces," *Antiques* CV (January 1974), 189.

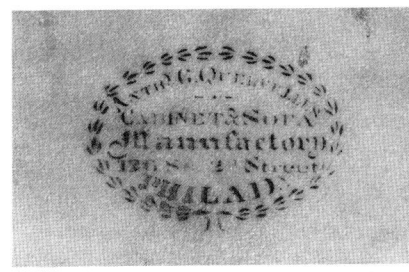

84

84a

85

86

85 Dresser and Mirror
New England or New York, ca. 1846
Pine, paint, reflective glass
H. 89¼ (226.70) W. 44 (111.76) D. 20¼ (51.44)
Society for the Preservation of New England
Antiquities, Boston, Massachusetts
1970.461 a, b

Evidently Henry Bowen was not as extravagant when he furnished Roseland's bedrooms as he was when he decorated the public rooms downstairs (for examples, see nos. 20 and 57). Graining on Bowen's chest concealed its humble pine origins. The maker even grained in a trompe l'oeil manner the sides and drawer fronts of the chest, implying framed panels. The arched mirror frame above is punctuated by a pierced quatrefoil revealing a trace of the mirror. The chest of drawers and its companion bed (no. 95) have mates that in later years were painted green. KSH

86 Dresser and Mirror*
United States, ca. 1846–1866
Black walnut, sugar maple, yellow poplar
H. 93 (236.22) W. 53½ (135.89) D. 26 (66.04)
National Museum of History and Technology,
Smithsonian Institution, Washington, D.C.
239,959

"A Gothic character may easily be given to plain chamber furniture by any joiner or cabinetmaker who has tools to make the necessary mouldings," wrote Andrew Jackson Downing.[1] Certainly this dresser and mirror are of such high quality that they were not made by just "any" cabinetmaker, although the dresser does illustrate how even a fairly plain design can be gothicized by the addition of a few columns and double-ended trefoil arches. The mirror, of course, is another matter. Its ornately domed shelves and heavily crocketed crest make a total statement that could not have been achieved merely by applying an overlay of ornament to a pre-existing form. The dresser, mirror, and a companion nightstand shared the same room in the Harral-Wheeler House as the bed (no. 97).[2] The dresser's greater refinement and its use of unpainted walnut, maple, and poplar imply that the grained bed may have been repainted to coordinate with the dresser but was not part of the same set. KSH

1. Andrew Jackson Downing, *The Architecture of Country Houses*, 443.
2. Anne Castrodale Golovin, *Bridgeport's Gothic Ornament: The Harral-Wheeler House*, 23.

87 Double Cabinet

Probably United States, ca. 1830–1850
Probably black walnut
H. 81 (205.74) W. 39½ (100.33) D. 19 (48.26)
The Keyes Foundation, New Orleans, Louisiana

Nothing could be more appropriate for an American romantic novelist than a Gothic Revival double cabinet. This cabinet was inherited by New Orleans mystery writer, Frances Parkinson Keyes, from her mother-in-law, Mrs. Henry Keyes.[1] Solid panels and a hemispherical upper section decorated with leafy crockets and an ornate finial relate this cabinet to a more ornate English derivative, the armoire designed by A. W. N. Pugin[2] and pictured here. KSH

1. Edith Gaines, ed., "Collectors' Notes," *Antiques* LXXXI (May 1962), 508.
2. Augustus Welby Northmore Pugin, *Gothic Furniture in the Style of the 15th Century*, pl. 3.

88 Hanging Wall Cabinet

Attributed to an unidentified ship's cabinetmaker
Long Island City, New York, ca. 1850–1860
Walnut, pine
H. 72¾ (184.79) W. 49¾ (126.37) D. 10½ (26.67)
Henry H. Livingston

This case, while at first glance reminiscent of Frances Parkinson Keyes's ornate cabinet, is nonetheless quite different. The case's simple but hardly naive, shallow, economical design illustrates the Gothic style at its most restrained. The two-door cabinet joins an austere six-drawer bracket below. Molded mullions enliven two lancet arches, which in reality are the cabinet doors. The cabinet's controlled, seemingly unique, design supports the family tradition that it was given to the owner's great-grandfather by one of his employees, a ship's cabinetmaker. Herman Thong (or Tong) Livingston (ca. 1826–1899) owned Livingston, Fox and Company, builders and owners of paddle-wheel steamers sailing between New York, New Orleans, and Havana in the third quarter of the nineteenth century. Their shipyard was in Long Island City where this cabinet presumably was made. KSH

89 Corner Whatnot*

New York, New York, ca. 1845–1850
Mahogany, mahogany veneer, reflective glass
H. 78 (198.12) W. 30 (76.20) D. 16 (40.64)
The Brooklyn Museum, Brooklyn, New York
52.132

The étagère or whatnot, one of the new forms of furniture introduced in the middle of the nineteenth century, rapidly became an indispensable item for the fashionably furnished parlor. This example, made to fit in a corner, relates to Andrew Jackson Downing's description of an "encoigneur," which he says was utilized "as a place for books, vases of flowers, and rare articles of *virtu* [sic]."[1] A nearly identical example, which must be from the same shop and bears traces of a New York City label, is in a private collection, and a third related whatnot is in the Vassall-Longfellow House in Cambridge, Massachusetts.[2] DBW

1. Andrew Jackson Downing, *The Architecture of Country Houses*, 435.
2. The privately owned piece has a torn label, which may be that of Gideon Sanford, 56 Beekman Street, New York. Sanford was at this address from 1845 to 1846. The Brooklyn Museum whatnot is illustrated in Helen Comstock, *American Furniture: Seventeenth, Eighteenth, and Nineteenth Century Styles*, no. 618.

90 Bookcase

Possibly Robert Renwick (active 1837–1890)
Baltimore, Maryland, ca. 1848
Rosewood, glass, mother-of-pearl escutcheons
H. 132 (336.28) W. 50 (127.00) D. 22 (55.88)
Maryland Historical Society, Baltimore, Maryland, Gift of Mrs. Henry Pratt Jones 48.9.1

Although this example has the standard rectangular shape of most bookcases, few others have ever been decorated with designs of such undulating fluidity. Its gallery, based on a series of circles and arcs, may not be "pointed," but it does convey a feeling of movement unmatched by other Gothic Revival ornament. Half-round, half-length clustered columns, robust finials, and scrollwork on the doors complete the requisite allusions to the Gothic.

This bookcase, which is one of a pair, has traditionally been attributed to Robert Renwick, a Baltimore cabinetmaker who was active alone from 1837 to 1865 and who then worked in partnership with his sons until 1890. Little is known about Renwick, and as yet no documentation supports the attribution. Originally intended for the parlor of the Enoch Pratt House, the bookcases may have been designed to fit in the recesses flanking the Gothic marble mantel there. Their fit would have been exact—were it not for the window and floor moldings, which reduced the space. KSH

91 Canopied Bed*

Possibly New Orleans, Louisiana, ca. 1845[1]
Mahogany, mahogany veneer
H. 116 (294.64) W. 63 (160.20) D. 86 (218.44)
Harris County Heritage Society, Houston, Texas 74.2

Canopied beds continued to be popular in the mid-nineteenth century, particularly in the deep South. At first glance this massive example appears to mix Restauration and Rococo motifs. A closer look reveals that in spite of its heavily framed ogee canopy and whimsically scalloped rails and headboard, the bed has an unmistakably Gothic Revival flavor. Octagonal posts stand on their original casters and rise to long classical columns, each embellished with two attenuated lancet arches. The footboard is actually topped by a progression of upright and inverted arches and the side rails, too, are sculpted with inverted arches. Each scallop on the conservative headboard terminates in a drop pendant and is separated from its neighbor by a crocket, thereby making the whole bed a subtle rather than an exuberant version of the Gothic Revival style. KSH

1. Peter M. Rippe, "Harris County Heritage Society of Houston," *Antiques* CVIII (September 1975), 494.

89

50

90

91

92

92 Bed

Probably United States, ca. 1840–1850
Mahogany, mahogany veneer, whitewood
Head H. 74 (198), Foot H. 60 (147) W. 70½ (180) D. 94½ (230)
Private Collection

The revivalist furniture designer often worked to ensure the archeological correctness of his products, but ironically there were few or no Gothic prototypes on which to base designs. As with the bed shown here, cabinetmakers had to turn to cathedrals, castles, and stained-glass window framing for sources. Here flamboyant arches like those used in the windows of the Chapel of Henry VII at Westminster Abbey are introduced on the head and footboards of the massive bed. Although the bed is "bristling with crockets,"[1] trefoil arches, and great hexagonal posts, its use of veneers and mahogany instead of oak, its high footboard, and its sheer massiveness ally it as closely to earlier Restauration styles as to pointed designs of the later revival. Its posts are drilled for casters and originally may have accommodated them.

KSH

1. Andrew Jackson Downing, *The Architecture of Country Houses*, 389.

93 Bed*

United States, before 1833
Pine
H. 103 (261.6) W. 66½ (168.9) D. 85 (215.9)
Mr. and Mrs. James Biddle

The jutting canopy of a half-tester bed provides an easily adaptable vehicle for the Gothic style. Brackets mark the cornice, Tudor arches span the tester, trefoil arches form an arcade across the headboard, and quatrefoils line up below it. An even more ornate frame marks the footboard. This bed has a long history with some interesting associations. It remains at Andalusia (see no. 183), the home once belonging to Nicholas Biddle, great-great-grandfather of the present owner. According to family tradition, the bed was given to Nicholas Biddle by Joseph Bonaparte in 1833 when Bonaparte gave up

93

Point Breeze in Bordentown, New Jersey, and returned to Europe. The bed, originally grained to resemble golden oak, has been repainted antique white within this century.[1]

KSH

1. *Antiques* LXXXI (May 1962), frontispiece, 503.

94 Bed*

Attributed to Crawford Riddell (active ca. 1837–1849)
Philadelphia, Pennsylvania, ca. 1837–1846
Rosewood
H. 162 (411.48) W. 90 (228.60) D. 104 (264.16)
David M. Underwood, Rosedown Plantation

In spite of the southern aristocrat's penchant for Greek Revival plantation homes, the planter frequently considered his way of life an idyllic version of the Middle Ages. Edward A. Pollard, that passionate newspaper editor/historian from Richmond, Virginia, preferred to downgrade "coarse and materialistic" Yankees in favor of "the colonists of Virginia and the Carolinas [who] were from the first distinguished by their polite manners, their fine sentiments, their attachment to a sort of feudal life, their landed gentry, their love of field-sports and dangerous adventure, and the prodigal and improvident aristocracy that dispensed its stores in constant rounds of hospitality and gaiety."[1]

Pollard may not have known that a New York Yankee, Andrew Jackson Downing, aggressively promoted "tasteful sensibilities" and medieval revival domiciles and that a Philadelphia cabinetmaker, Crawford Riddell, was associated with the monumental bedroom suite in the Gothic style now at Rosedown Plantation in Saint Francisville, Louisiana. Rosedown was built in the Greek style in 1835 by Daniel and Martha Turnbull, who by family tradition acquired this gigantic bed, six chairs, two washstands, one armoire, and a bureau from Crawford Riddell. Tradition continues that the bed had been intended for Henry Clay's use in the White House had he been elected president in 1844. Since no room at Rosedown could accommodate a bed that towered thirteen and one-half feet, Turnbull had to build a room to house it. The bed is not labeled; however, two of the washstands bear the stencil: "CRAW-

52

94

FORD RIDDELL'S / JOURNEYMEN CABINET MAKERS / FURNITURE WARE-HOUSE / 48. S. FIFTH ST / PHILAD." Philadelphia city directories show Riddell operating at this location between 1837 and 1846.

1. Edward A. Pollard, *The Lost Cause; A New Southern History of the Confederates* (New York: E. B. Treat and Co., 1866), 51, 50.

95   Bed
      Probably New England or New York, ca. 1846
      White pine, paint
      H. 47½ (120.65)   W. 60¼ (153.04)   L. 85½ (217.17)
      Society for the Preservation of New England Antiquities, Boston, Massachusetts
      1970.460

Like its matching chest-of-drawers (no. 85), this grained bed is far less pretentious than the Gothic furnishings that Henry C. Bowen ordered for the public rooms in Roseland. The bed and its twin, which has since been painted green, are as much updated Restauration sleigh beds as they are examples of the newer Gothic style.   KSH

96   Bed
      Possibly designed by Alexander Jackson Davis (1803–1892)
      New York, New York, ca. 1841–1866
      Oak
      H. 91 (231.14)   W. 66 (167.64)   D. 86 (218.44)
      Lyndhurst, National Trust for Historic Preservation, Tarrytown, New York
      NT 64.25.495

Few Gothic Revival furnishings are as handsome, as monumental, or as elusive as this bed used by Helen Gould Shepard, daughter of Jay Gould, the financier who bought Lyndhurst in 1880.[1] This bed and the one from the Harral-Wheeler House (no. 97) are so similar as to be almost certainly by the same hand. Lyndhurst was designed by Alexander Jackson Davis for William and Philip R. Paulding in 1838–1841 and remodeled by him for George Merritt in 1864–1867, and the Harral-Wheeler House was designed by Davis in 1846–1848 for Henry Kollock Harral. However, no Davis drawing identical to either of these beds survives.[2]

The following, therefore, can be said with some surety: there is no surviving Davis material to indicate that Davis ever designed any movable furniture for Henry K. Harral, nor is there any surviving material indicating that Davis ever designed any beds for George Merritt; Davis does mention designing a bed for Paulding; and Davis's son, Joseph Beale Davis, contradicts the above by writing that his

95

96

father provided bedroom suites for George Merritt.[3] No matter who designed or made these great beds, they are as close as any to the bed illustrated by Andrew Jackson Downing in *Country Houses* and are two of the most successful known attempts of the American Gothic Revival.[4] KSH

1. *Lyndhurst, On the Hudson River, Tarrytown, N.Y.*, 40.
2. Stanley Mallach, "Gothic Furniture Designs by Alexander Jackson Davis," 121, 123.
3. Joseph Beale Davis, "American Furniture," manuscript in the Alexander Jackson Davis Papers, Avery Architectural Library, Columbia University, New York, reprinted in *ibid.*, 132.
4. Andrew Jackson Downing, *The Architecture of Country Houses*, 447.

97   Bed*
     Possibly designed by Alexander Jackson Davis
        (1803–1892)
     New York, New York, ca. 1840–1850
     White pine, yellow poplar, paint
     H. 103¼ (262.26) W. 68½ (178.99) D. 87½
        (121.45)
     National Museum of History and Technology,
        Smithsonian Institution, Washington, D.C.
                                           239,959

The relationship between this bed and Lyndhurst's great bed (no. 96) is obvious, both in general design and in such specific elements as the headboard, flanking posts, and footboards with applied shields. As previously noted, only stylistic similarities and the coincidence that both beds were in country houses designed by Alexander Jackson Davis link the two. As with other Harral-Wheeler House furniture, the bed was originally painted to resemble oak. At a later date maple and walnut graining were applied to this base layer. KSH

98   Crib
     United States, ca. 1835–1845
     Black walnut
     H. 44½ (113.03) W. 41¼ (104.78) D. 29½ (74.93)
     Mr. Stephen Parks, New Haven, Connecticut

"*Cribs* are bedsteads for children so young as to render it unsafe to trust them by themselves in beds with unguarded sides. They are generally intended to be placed, during the night, by the bedside of the mother; and, for that purpose, the height of the crib should correspond with that of the large bed, and one of its sides be made to lift out," wrote John Claudius Loudon when he illustrated two cribs in his encyclopedia.[1] This crib, which at one time was fitted with slats to support its mattress and casters for ease of movement, offered an infant his own fortification. It thereby served him in much the same way that prototypic medieval castles served his European ancestors. The crib was acquired from a dealer who said he bought it privately in Virginia in 1962. KSH

1. John Claudius Loudon, *An Encyclopædia of Cottage, Farm, and Villa Architecture and Furniture*, reprinted in *Furniture for the Victorian Home* (Watkins Glen, New York: American Life Foundation, 1968), 123.

99   Child's Bedstead
     Noyes and Hutton (active partnership ca.
        1848–1852)
     Troy, New York, 1851–1852
     Cast iron
     H. 35 (88.90) W. 57½ (146.05) D. 37½ (95.25)
     David Allen Hanks, Philadelphia, Pennsylvania

Cast iron made sturdy, efficient, and mass produced furniture; in other words, it was the perfect material for a child's bed. Moreover, Gothic Revival quatrefoils and interlacing arches suited cast iron, providing a degree of decoration that was both stylish and economical to produce. The bed is labeled on the inside top rail of each end: "NOYES & HUTTON / PATENT'D SEP'T 1851." According to the *Annual Report of the Commissioners of Patents* (1851), Pelatiah M. Hutton of Troy, New York, took out a design patent (No. 407) for a cast-iron bedstead on September 2, 1851. Noyes and Hutton first appear in Troy city directories in 1848-1849 as the owners of a "Hollow Ware Foundry, on the Pier south of Adams street." They must have prospered because in 1851-1852 they are listed as "Noyes & Hutton, hollow ware foundry, all kinds of stove ware, tea kettles, cast iron bedsteads, &c., 119 river." By 1852-1853 Hutton had withdrawn from the firm, which then operated under the name of Noyes and Tillman. In all probability this bed was made between 1851 and 1852.

KSH

100 Pier Glass

Probably Philadelphia, Pennsylvania, ca. 1830-1840
Mahogany veneer, pine, reflective glass
H. 56 (142.24) W. 20 (50.80) D. 2½ (6.35)
Mr. Lee B. Anderson

This early Restoration pier glass with ogee arch and flanking columns is a continuation of the architectural, tabernacle-frame looking glasses made in Philadelphia in the first quarter of the nineteenth century.[1] In addition, the design of the leaf capitals, a new element, conforms to Philadelphia carving of the Empire period,[2] further strengthening an attribution to the city that is suggested by a history of ownership there.

DBW

1. Charles F. Montgomery, *American Furniture: The Federal Period*, 283.
2. Robert C. Smith, "Philadelphia Empire Furniture by Antoine Gabriel Quervelle," *Antiques* LXXXVI (September 1964), 309, fig. 13.

101 Mirror

Possibly United States, ca. 1830-1840
Basswood, gilt over gesso, reflective glass
H. 32 (81.28) W. 16 (40.64) D. 1 (2.54)
Mr. Stephen Parks, New Haven, Connecticut

By the 1830s the term "looking glass" was abandoned in favor of the simpler "mirror." With almost feminine delicacy this mirror exhibits a full vocabulary of Gothic Revival ornament from its long, thin, paired columns and low Tudor arch to galleries of repeated trefoil arches below and above the glass. The mirror was acquired by its present owner in Virginia.

KSH

102 Dressing Glass

United States, ca. 1840-1850
Mahogany, reflective glass
H. 44 (111.76) W. 24 (60.96) D. 9¾ (24.77)
Mr. Lee B. Anderson

Without any sacrifice of form or function, the maker of this dressing glass, with its flamboyant arch between buttress-like spires, has achieved a remarkably architectural form. The small clustered columns closing the composition at either end of the serpentine drawer are a particularly attractive detail. The piece has a history of ownership on Long Island.

DBW

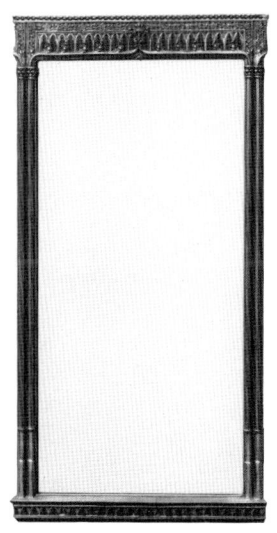

103

103 Overmantel Mirror*

Probably New York or New England, ca. 1846–1866
Gilt over unidentified base material, reflective glass
H. 66 (167.64) W. 72 (182.88) D. 7 (17.78)
National Museum of History and Technology, Smithsonian Institution, Washington, D.C.
239,959

Gothic Revival overmantel mirrors are far rarer than examples made in the Rococo style. This mirror once graced the Gothic bedroom in the Harral-Wheeler House (no. 185). Its relationship to the dresser and mirror in the same room (no. 86) is obvious, although its quality of execution is not as fine. Interestingly, three-socket Rococo sconces are subsituted for the more expected shelves below the gilt hoods.   KSH

104 Cheval Glass

United States, ca. 1835–1850
Oak, reflective glass
H. 78 (198.12) W. 32 (81.28) D. 14 (35.56)
Mr. Lee B. Anderson

While introduced at the end of the eighteenth century the cheval glass remained a rare and luxurious form of furniture as late as the time this Gothic example was made. According to Rudolph Ackermann's *Repository* (1827): "Great attention must be paid, in designing this piece of furniture, to give it a frame sufficiently solid to support the weight of so large a glass without appearing heavy and ponderous."[1] Here the cabinetmaker has adopted the basic window form with a little tracery above, has crenelated the skirt, and has crocketed the legs, thereby achieving with great success a cheval glass that conforms to Ackermann's precepts. While oral tradition states that this cheval glass was used at Point Breeze, the Bordentown, New Jersey, home of Joseph Bonaparte, it does not relate stylistically to the documented bed with that provenance now at Andalusia (no. 93).[2]   DBW

1. "Gothic Looking Glass," in Rudolph Ackermann, ed., *The Repository of Arts, Literature, Fashions, Manufactures, etc.*, January 1827, p. 60.
2. *Antiques* LXXXI (May 1962), 502.

104

105 Pier Glass*

Possibly Alexander Jackson Davis (1803–1892)
New York, New York, ca. 1857
Possibly mahogany, reflective glass
H. (excluding finials) 113 (287.02) W. 51 (129.54) D. 7 (17.78)
St. Christopher's School, Dobbs Ferry, New York

It is rare to find an original pair of mirrors still in their original nineteenth-century home, but it is rarer still to find them in a home that has served as a boarding school since 1890. In 1857 Davis designed two "mirror frames" (presumably like the one shown here, although no drawing survives) for Ingleside (now St. Christopher's), the home he had designed for Edwin B. Strange in 1854–1855. "California marble slabs" to go under them were purchased from Fisher and Company of New York.[1] The finials, crockets, and crest rails on this mirror are very similar to those on the bed from the Harral-Wheeler House (no. 97). The half section, hexagonal columns and rosettes on the sides enhance the mirror's Gothic mood and appropriately complement the Gothic air underscored throughout Ingleside.   KSH

1. Jane B. Davies, "St. Christopher's School, Dobbs Ferry, The Main Building," notes written May 30, 1974, and available through the school.

106 Hall Stand

Attributed to Thomas Brooks (1811–1887)
Brooklyn, New York, ca. 1846
White oak, reflective glass, cast iron
H. 88 (221.52) W. 30¼ (76.83) D. 16½ (41.91)
Society for the Preservation of New England Antiquities, Boston, Massachusetts
1970.423 a, b

The hall stand is part of the furnishings made for the Bowens of Roseland in Woodstock, Connecticut (see nos. 186 and 20) and attributed to Thomas Brooks. In affect the maker has elongated the back of a Gothic Revival settee (no. 56) while introducing hat hooks, a mirror, and an umbrella rest to the frame. Perhaps more noteworthy than the stand were the people who used it. Henry Bowen was an ardent Republican whose Fourth of July gatherings were well known. At one such party on July 4, 1889, with the lawns "illuminated with lanterns and the piazzas decorated with bunting and flags," there was an "irreverent rain," which no doubt dampened the stand and the spirit of the principal guest, President Benjamin Harrison.[1]   KSH

1. The *New York Herald* (July 4, 1889) and the *New York Times* (July 5, 1889) as quoted in Polly Rabinowitz, "Life at Roseland: Bowens and Holts," 12.

107 Hall Stand

United States, ca. 1851–1855
Oak, marble, reflective glass, cast iron
H. 102 (259.10) W. 50½ (128.20) D. 16½ (41.80)
The Estate of Mrs. Hubert F. Barnum, Natchez, Mississippi

Few products of the Gothic Revival style are quite as exuberant in design as this stand, which was probably made by the same shop as the hall chairs formerly at Stanton Hall in Natchez, Mississippi (no. 48),[1] and shares with them identical front legs, stiles, skirt, and finials. The stand bristles with protruding hat hooks and rounded trefoils atop flamboyant arches.   KSH

1. Celia Jackson Otto, *American Furniture of the Nineteenth Century*, 120.

108 Hall Stand

United States, ca. 1840–1850
Rosewood, marble, cast iron, reflective glass
H. 92¾ (235.58) W. 45 (114.30) D. 17 (43.18)
On loan from the Smithsonian Institution Furnishings Collection, Washington, D.C.
SI 70.169

When the American edition of the *Encyclopædia of Domestic Economy* first appeared (1849) it counseled readers in everything from furnishings and cooking to hygiene. Among various household amenities the authors thoughtfully listed furniture suitable to the hall and staircase: "Door scrapers and brush./Cloak and hat stands./Cloak rails./Umbrella drains./Chairs./Benches./Floor cloth./Stair carpet and rods./Mats./Letterbox./Lamps./ [and] Stove."[1] Certainly this hall stand would be an efficient addition to any

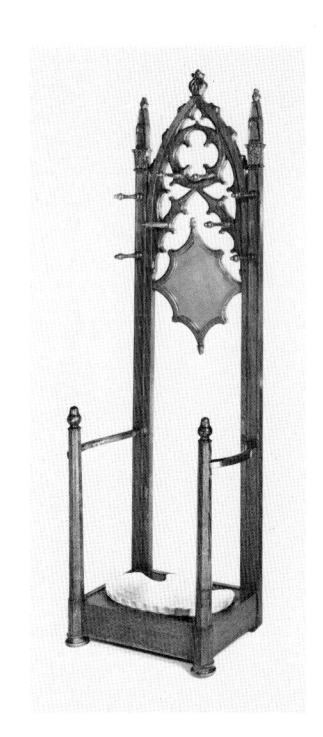

105

106

107

108

hall, although its hat hooks, drawer, marble shelf, mirror, and cast-iron umbrella drains seem lost to the heavy ogee arch above. KSH

1. Thomas Webster and Mrs. [William] Parkes, *An Encyclopædia of Domestic Economy*, 313.

109 Hall Stand

Probably United States, ca. 1850–1870
Walnut, cast iron, reflective glass
H. 87¼ (221.62) W. 31¾ (80.65) D. 15¼ (38.74)
From the collections of the Louisiana State Museum, New Orleans, Louisiana 1967.53

Walnut clustered columns, refined arches, and a trefoil above the cast-iron drip pan imply that this hall stand was made in the middle of the century. However, the pierced latticework at its midsection, the round mirror, the design constrained by the margins of the structure itself, and the rather squat arch all suggest the styles endorsed by Charles Eastlake and point to a later date of manufacture. KSH

110 Reed Organ

Possibly by John Percival
Auburn, New York, ca. 1850
Mahogany, mahogany veneer, satinwood case
H. 36¼ (92.08) W. 45¼ (114.94) D. 23¼ (59.06)
Collections of Greenfield Village and the Henry Ford Museum, Dearborn, Michigan
00.3.3691

Reed organs are keyboard wind instruments in which air is blown over a set of reeds to produce a sound, rather than forced through pipes. They are, of course, much less expensive and much more portable than standard pipe organs. This little organ possesses an attractively veneered case of the pillar and scroll type, but inserted on either side of the keyboard are two unmistakable Gothic arches, a motif that is repeated in the music stand. Because of similar mechanisms and cases, this instrument has been associated with a labeled example in the same collection made by John Percival of Auburn, New York. Percival advertised in Auburn city directories in the 1850s as the operator of a music store and the maker of pianofortes. KSH

111 Door and Door Frame†

Designed by Alexander Jackson Davis (1803–1892)
Probably designed in New York, New York, ca. 1846
Unidentified wood, paint
National Museum of History and Technology, Smithsonian Institution, Washington, D.C.

"Good examples of this [Gothic] mode of treating bedrooms may be seen in the very complete villa of Mr. Harold [sic], at Bridgeport, Ct., built from the Designs of Mr. Davis," wrote Andrew Jackson Downing.[1] Like most Gothic country houses, the Harral-Wheeler House was truthful to its style both inside and out. Doors, door frames, corbels, window frames, and moldings carried the Gothic theme throughout the house. In spite of a great preservation effort, the Harral-Wheeler House was demolished in 1958. The door and door frame, many other architectural elements, and one period room were salvaged by the Smithsonian Institution. KSH

1. Andrew Jackson Downing, *The Architecture of Country Houses*, 386.
† Not illustrated.

112 Steeple Clock

Forestville Manufacturing Company (1835–1855)
Forestville, Connecticut, ca. 1845–1855
Rosewood veneer, paint, glass
H. 19 (48.3) W. 12⅛ (30.8) D. 4 (10.2)
Collections of Greenfield Village and the Henry Ford Museum, Dearborn, Michigan
00.4.1724

By the 1830s inexpensive shelf clocks had largely replaced more stately tall-case examples in American homes. Companies like the Forestville Manufacturing Company proliferated in Connecticut, where an incredible number of shelf clocks were produced, many of which were exported to England. This steeple clock is one of the more ornate Gothic products. Its heavily carved frame, graceful arch, and free-standing columns make this clock a fine example of its type. Jonathan Clark Brown (1807–1872) established the Forestville Manufacturing Company in 1835. After two name changes between 1840 and 1847 the company returned to its former name. This clock is labeled "FORESTVILLE MANUFACTURING CO. / J. C. BROWN." The company continued until 1855 when losses from a fire two years earlier led to its demise.[1]   KSH

1. Brooks Palmer, "Acorn Clocks," *Antiques* LV (March 1949), 192–194.

113 Clock
   American Clock Company (active ca. 1835–1855)
   New York, New York, ca. 1850
   Cast iron and other metals, glass, wood
   H. 21⅝ (54.99) W. 13½ (34.29) D. 4½ (11.43)
   Collections of Greenfield Village and the Henry Ford Museum, Dearborn, Michigan
   00.3.3445

This clock is less complicated than it appears. The remarkable cast-iron case is really no more than a façade, and behind its black body, green figures, urns, and leafage, rust steps and spires, and white classical temple is a simple wooden box containing the clock's works.[1] The paper label inside its wooden back reads: "MANUFACTURED AND SOLD BY THE / AMERICAN CLOCK COMPANY, / DEPOT, 3 CORTLANDT STREET, / NEW YORK." Raised letters cast on the back of the façade report: "BRADLEY & / HUBBARD / PATENT / APPLIED FOR, 1850." The American Clock Company was owned by Franklin C. Andrews. Although Andrews first appears in New York city directories in 1845 as a purveyor of clocks, the American Clock Company is not listed until 1851. Both Andrews and his company remained active at 3 Cortlandt Street into the 1860s.   KSH

1. Helen Comstock, *American Furniture: Seventeenth, Eighteenth, and Nineteenth Century Styles*, 309.

114 Mantel Set
   United States, ca. 1840–1850
   Gilt on metal, marble, cut glass
   Center standard: H. 18½ (46.99) W. 16¼ (41.28) D. 3⅞ (9.84)
   Side standards: H. 15¾ (40.01) W. 6¼ (15.88) D. 3½ (8.89)
   The Fine Arts Museums of San Francisco, San Francisco, California   X 71.130 a, b, c

A knight, perhaps Sir Walter Scott's Ivanhoe or Alfred, Lord Tennyson's Lancelot, a saint, or simply a romantic rendering of a bygone hero stands within the elaborate Rococo Revival framework of this mantel set. Implicit here is the domestication of the medieval Gothic taste brought into the parlors of fashionable nineteenth-century homes. Although the maker cannot be identified, it is interesting to note that the cast oval ring from which the lusters are suspended seems identical to the rings on William F. Shaw's Boston candlesticks (no. 115).   KSH

113

114

112

61

115a

115

116

117

115 Pair of Candlesticks

William F. Shaw (active ca. 1845–1900)
Boston, Massachusetts, ca. 1848–1851
Gilt on brass, marble, cut glass
H. 14 (35.56) W. 6½ (16.51) D. 3½ (8.90)
Mr. Charles V. Swain

Mount Auburn Cemetery in Cambridge, Massachusetts, six miles from Boston, opened in 1831. As America's first planned, landscaped burying ground, it was referred to by Andrew Jackson Downing as "the Athens of New England," a park suitable for afternoon strolls as well as for burying the dead.[1] It is not surprising that the Bigelow Chapel at Mount Auburn would become the subject for decorative candlesticks, nor is it surprising that the candlesticks would be made in Boston.[2] Cast on the back of each base are the words "W. F. SHAW / 270 WASH'N ST / BOSTON / PATENT / DEC 18 1848." William F. Shaw is first listed in the 1845 Boston city directory. He moved to 270 Washington Street in 1848 and remained there through 1851. Two other sets with identical standards are known, one of which has a stepped marble base and a center three-socket candelabrum.[3]

KSH

1. Andrew Jackson Downing, *Rural Essays*, edited by George William Curtis, 154.
2. Joseph T. Butler, *Candleholders in America, 1650–1900*, 137.
3. One set belongs to Sleepy Hollow Restorations, Tarrytown, New York, the other to Joan and Bruce Bogart.

116 Pair of Argand Lamps

Sold by Clark, Coit, and Cargill (active partnership ca. 1833–1836)
New York, New York, 1833–1836
Cast bronze, glass shades
H. 25 (63.50) W. 5½ (13.97)
Mr. Lee B. Anderson

Although Ami Argand first patented Argand lamps in France in 1783, they did not come into popular use in the United States until the second quarter of the nineteenth century.[1] Argand lamps are distinguished by their cylindrical wicks which are saturated by fuel on the outside and which channel air on the inside, thus creating a clean, bright light. These hexagonal lamps with standards and fonts reminiscent of Gothic reliquaries are stamped on the burner with the name "Clark, Coit, and Cargill." According to New York city directories William Starr Clark and Henry A. Cargill operated a "furnishing store" in the early 1830s at 9 Maiden Lane. Cargill is listed in the 1833–1834 Longworth's *Almanac* as working in a "lamp store." In the 1833–1834 directory the men were joined by Thomas C. Coit in a partnership that lasted until 1836–1837 when Cargill withdrew from the firm. In all probability these lamps were made between 1833 and 1836, but whether the firm actually produced them or merely retailed them is not known.

KSH

1. C. Malcolm Watkins, "Lighting Devices," in Helen Comstock, ed., *The Concise Encyclopedia of American Antiques*, 359–360.

117 Astral Lamp

United States, ca. 1840–1855
Brass, tin, glass
H. 26⅛ (66.36) W. 5⅞ (14.92) D. 5⅞ (14.92)
The Bayou Bend Collection, The Museum of Fine Arts, Houston, Texas   B.68.24

Astral lamps with their shadowless light were first patented as table lamps by the Frenchman Bordier-Marcet in 1810.[1] By the second quarter of the nineteenth century they were in frequent use in fashionable American homes. Like contemporary furniture, this lamp exhibits the introduction of Gothic Revival ornamentation within a classical framework. An almost exotic trefoil arch appears on each side of its square plinth, offering simple relief to an otherwise severely classical design. KSH

1. Leroy Thwing, *Flickering Flames: A History of Domestic Lighting through the Ages*, (Rutland, Vt.: Charles E. Tuttle Co., 1958), 75–76.

118 Astral Lamp

Cornelius and Company (active partnership 1840–1855)
Philadelphia, Pennsylvania, 1849–1855
Bronze, glass
H. 24 (60.96) W. 8 (20.32)
Joan and Bruce Bogart

In 1857 John F. Watson wrote in the *Annals of Philadelphia* that "Mr. Cornelius now makes the most elegant mantel and hanging lamps; his manner of *succeeding* in that, and in *silver plating*, is a *very curious history*, and would deserve to be well told at great length."[1] This astral lamp, labeled "CORNELIUS & CO. / PHILAD / JULY 24th 1849 / PATENT / APRIL 18th 1843," is no exception. Beginning at its flaired, heavily foliated base, which is certainly more Rococo than Gothic, moving up its narrow standard ornamented with a delicate "Gothick" arch, and continuing to its shoulder softened by fragile drops, this lamp is stable, relatively streamlined, and visually satisfying. The lamp is further enhanced by a spherical cut-glass shade that successfully adapts graduated arches to its shape. It is the product of Christian Cornelius, a Dutchman who arrived in Philadelphia in 1783. Cornelius began working as a silversmith (1810), became a silver plater and patent lamp manufacturer (1825), and later operated under the name of Cornelius and Company. He left a dynasty of lampmakers who worked late into the nineteenth century. Appropriately, one of their later catalogues (circa 1875) shows that they were influenced by the Gothic Revival designs of Charles Eastlake.[2] KSH

1. *Lamps & Other Lighting Devices, 1850–1906*, 21.
2. Ibid., 23–44.

118

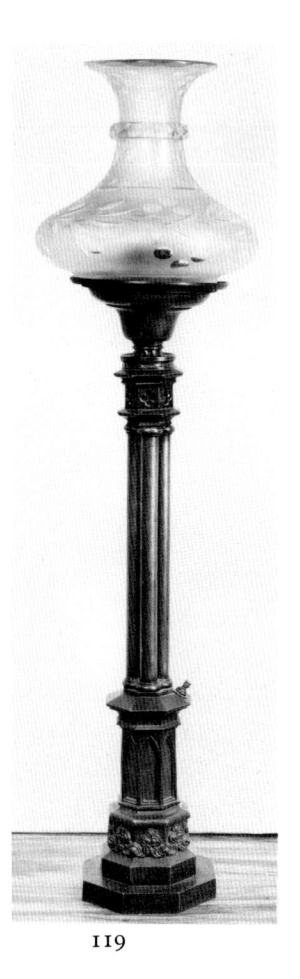

119 **Astral Lamp**
Probably United States, ca. 1840–1855
Bronze, glass
H. 25½ (64.77) DIAM. 6 (15.24)
Mr. Lee B. Anderson

Unlike the previous lamp (no. 117), this astral lamp is completely dominated by the Gothic order. From its stepped octagonal base with a gallery of arches to the top of its clustered columns, every ornament reinforces its Gothic Revival intent. KSH

120 **Kerosene Oil Lamp**
Probably United States, after 1854
White metal, glass
H. (without chimney) 22 (55.88) W. 7¼ (18.42)
Joan and Bruce Bogart

This ornate lamp by an unknown maker is a happy blend of nineteenth century technology, Gothic Revival frills, and Rococo ornamentation. Developed in 1854, kerosene was the last major fuel used for lighting devices before the gas age.[1] Neither the Gothic Revival arches surrounding this lamp's kerosene font nor the elaborate, repeated, flamboyant arches and drops on its skirt contribute to the structural design of the lamp. Nor do they relate to the Rococo cherubs' heads on each foot and the shells on the dome. In spite of its inverted sense of proportion and inconsistency of decorative modes, the lamp is certainly an endearing representative of its type. In all probability the shade decorated with the Greek key motif is a later addition. An identical lamp in another collection appears to have its original shade complete with flamboyant arches and trefoils. KSH

1. C. Malcolm Watkins, "Lighting Devices," in Helen Comstock, ed., *The Concise Encyclopedia of American Antiques*, 361–362.

121 **Pitcher**
Attributed to the New England Glass Company
Boston, Massachusetts, ca. 1825–1840
Glass
H. 7⅛ (18.10) W. 7¼ (18.50)
The Corning Museum of Glass, Corning, New York   55.4.222

This quart pitcher, like others of the "blown three-mold" type, received its ornamentation when the glassblower blew his colorless glass into a three-part mold, thereby impressing a gallery of repeat lancet arches on its side. It is incidental that the blower used a decanter mold for his design. Glass is so malleable in its molten state that he could work it into almost any shape he pleased—and then apply the handle to the completed form.[1] KSH

1. The pitcher and its sister decanters are from the GIV-6 mold, a glass collector's term indicating that they were all produced in the same factory from the same mold. George S. McKearin and Helen McKearin, *American Glass*, 321.

122　Decanter

Attributed to the Boston and Sandwich Glass Company
Boston, Massachusetts, after 1825
Glass
H. 11 (27.94) W. 4⅞ (12.40)
Collections of Greenfield Village and the Henry Ford Museum, Dearborn, Michigan
59.28.244A–B

Like the pitcher (no. 121) this quart whiskey decanter was fabricated in a "blown three-mold" pattern. This particular decanter and five similar molds, which bear the labels "RUM," "GIN," "BRANDY," "CHERRY [sic]," and "WINE," comprise an identifiable pattern family.[1] Each has an arch- and fern-decorated body and a snake medallion framing the name of the demon spirit inside. Fragments of similar clear glass decanters have been found on the site of the Boston and Sandwich Glass factory, which opened its doors in 1825.[2]　KSH

1. The pattern is GIV-7 (see George S. McKearin and Helen McKearin, *American Glass*, 297).
2. Ibid., 146.

123　Window Pane

Pittsburgh Flint Glass Manufactory of Bakewell and Company (1808–1882)
Pittsburgh, Pennsylvania, after 1825
Glass
H. 7 (17.6) W. 5 (12.5)
The Corning Museum of Glass, Corning, New York
56.4.10

In 1825 Bakewell and Company of Pittsburgh added pressed-glass products to its successful lines of blown and flint glass.[1] Some time not long afterwards it must have made this finely detailed, clear, pressed-glass pane labeled "BAKEWELL" on the reverse center. Since this small pane exhibits a complete vocabulary of Gothic ornament (clustered columns, crenelations, rosettes, and two types of arches), it may have dressed up a much more conservative frame.　KSH

1. George S. McKearin and Helen McKearin, *American Glass*, 139.

124　Compote

Attributed to the Boston and Sandwich Glass Company
Boston, Massachusetts, ca. 1830–1840
Glass
H. 6⅛ (15.5) DIAM. 10½ (26.6)
The St. Louis Art Museum, St. Louis, Missouri: Bequest of Christine Graham Long
435:1961.2

Hearts were popular decorative devices on lacy pressed glass, and it was not uncommon to see them combined with Gothic arches in a nineteenth-century design (see no. 128).[1] Here hearts and leaves alternate in a diapered band above a clear bowl of lancet arches and ribbed fans.　KSH

1. For examples of four heart and quatrefoil lacy pressed glass cup plates, see George S. McKearin and Helen McKearin, *American Glass*, pl. 187.

125　Dish

Attributed to the Boston and Sandwich Glass Company
Boston, Massachusetts, ca. 1840
Glass
H. 1½ (3.81) W. 5¼ (13.34) L. 7¼ (18.42)
Collections of Greenfield Village and the Henry Ford Museum, Dearborn, Michigan
00.3.7596

Arches and fans gracefully adapt themselves to the oval sides of this shallow dish. In doing so they establish a continuing relationship of curves between the shape of the dish and the interplay of ovals within its base. This clear example was mass-produced from a lacy pressed pattern mold.　KSH

123

124

125

126   Dish

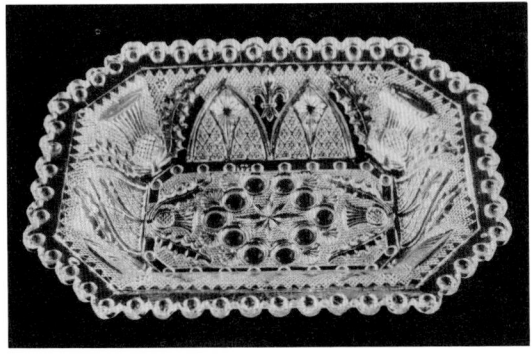

    Attributed to the Boston and Sandwich Glass Company
    Boston, Massachusetts, ca. 1835
    Glass
    H. 1 5/16 (2.85) W. 6 1/16 (14.39) D. 4 7/16 (11.23)
    Collections of Greenfield Village and the Henry Ford Museum, Dearborn, Michigan
    00.145.31

The study of lacy pressed glass is intriguing because many patterns seem superficially identical but in reality are from different molds and may, indeed, be from different factories. This oblong dish is just such an example. There are at least two other Leaf and Gothic Arch patterns virtually identical to this and two more Gothic Arch patterns that differ principally in their floral details.[1] That the particular motif should be so frequently reproduced is a testimonial to the popularity of the Gothic Revival style.

KSH

1. George S. McKearin and Helen McKearin, *American Glass*, pl. 150.

127   Dish

    Probably Middle West, ca. 1830–1840
    Glass
    H. 1 1/2 (3.8) W. 5 1/4 (13.4) L. 6 7/8 (17.5)
    The Corning Museum of Glass, Corning, New York
    58.4.60

At first glance, this clear, lacy, pressed-glass dish seems to be a very conventional example of its type, but a second glance shows that it is full of romantic medieval references: the sides are ornamented with lancet arches; thistles, the heraldic symbol for the royal badge of Scotland, mark each corner and the base of the dish; and two small fleur-de-lis, adopted by Louis VII of France as his royal emblem, punctuate two sides.

KSH

128   Covered Dish on a Tray

    Attributed to the Boston and Sandwich Glass Company
    Boston, Massachusetts, ca. 1830–1840
    Glass
    Tray: H. 1 (2.54) W. 4 1/2 (11.43) D. 7 (17.78)
    Overall: H. 5 (12.70) W. 4 (10.16) D. 6 3/8 (16.21)
    Collections of Greenfield Village and the Henry Ford Museum, Dearborn, Michigan
    3.580A-B-C

Arches on the sides and on the stepped lid of this clear, lacy, pressed, covered dish suggest more a medieval tomb than a container fit for a table. The complexity of design and attention to detail are perhaps most apparent at the dish's intricately molded edges.

KSH

129   Covered Sugar Bowl

    Probably Middle West, ca. 1830–1845
    Glass
    H. (with cover) 6 1/4 (15.9) DIAM. 5 (12.7)
    The Corning Museum of Glass, Corning, New York
    65.4.46

Neither America's Gothic Revival nor the manufacture of sugar bowls was restricted to the East Coast. This clear, lacy, pressed-glass sugar bowl probably comes from a midwestern glass house that was operating between 1830 and 1845.

KSH

130 Three Sugar Bowls

Attributed to the Boston and Sandwich Glass Company
Boston, Massachusetts, ca. 1835–1845
Glass
H. (with cover) 5½ (13.97) W. 4¾ (12.07)
New Haven Colony Historical Society, New Haven, Connecticut
1970.221, 222, and 225

Octagonal pressed-glass sugar bowls were among the most popular Gothic Revival glass forms made. These stout bowls, which vaguely resemble baptismal fonts, were made in a multitude of colors, including clear glass, "vaseline, canary yellow, light peacock blue, varying degrees of opalescence, opaque white, moonstone, turquoise-blue, sapphire-blue, deep amethyst, [and] deep emerald-green."[1] Each bowl and lid bears four different lancet-arch patterns, each repeated twice. KSH

1. George S. McKearin and Helen McKearin, *American Glass*, 363, pl. 163.

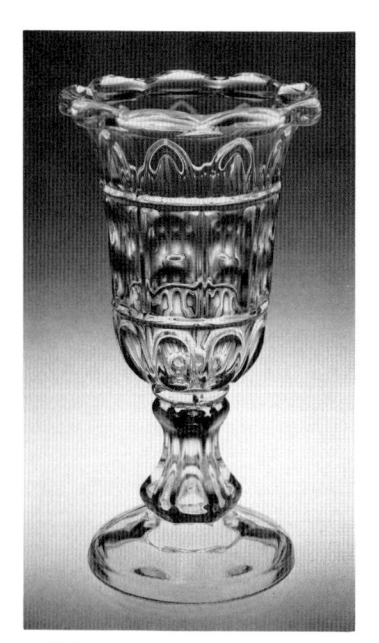

131 **Salt Dish**

Probably United States, ca. 1840
Glass
H. 2¼ (5.72) DIAM. 3 (7.62)
Collections of Greenfield Village and the Henry Ford Museum, Dearborn, Michigan
30.1448.14

A gather of glass was rammed into a mold to make this clear, pressed-glass, footed salt. Its stout crenelated base supports a simple bowl framed in lancet arches. KSH

132 **Salt Dish**

Probably New England, ca. 1830–1840
Glass
H. 1½ (3.9) W. 2⅛ (5.4) L. 2⅞ (7.2)
The Corning Museum of Glass, Corning, New York
59.4.53

Small, rectangular, footed salts such as this were common items on better dining tables in the nineteenth century. This example was machine made: a gather of glass was pressed into a full-sized mold; it was not manipulated by hand once it was removed from the mold. This salt in the Gothic Arch pattern, and others like it in opalescent lavender-blue, probably came from the New England area and were made between 1830 and 1840.[1] KSH

1. George S. McKearin and Helen McKearin, *American Glass*, 370–371.

133 **Celery Vase**

Attributed to the McKee Factory
Pittsburgh, Pennsylvania, after 1850
Glass
H. 10 (25.40) DIAM. 5½ (13.97)
Mrs. Stanley Hanks

Pressed loops at the base of the bowl, printed panels at the waist, and Gothic arches around the rim of this clear, nine-sided celery vase resemble the design of others attributed to the McKee Factory. James and Frederick McKee established their factory in 1850.[1] KSH

1. George S. McKearin and Helen McKearin, *American Glass*, 607.

134 **Sauce Bottle**

Probably United States, ca. 1850–1860
Soda lime glass
H. 8¾ (22.23) DIAM. 2⅜ (6.05)
Collections of Greenfield Village and the Henry Ford Museum, Dearborn, Michigan
00.3.12930

According to their present-day labels, Brand's Steak Sauce was declared "A.1." at the 1862 London Exposition and Tabasco Sauce originated before 1868 on Avery Island in Louisiana. These modern sauces are but two survivors of the many seasonings that proliferated in nineteenth-century America. The revivalist sauce bottle pictured here was molded from clear aquamarine glass in the middle of the century. Unlike some decorative styles that remained the privileges of the upper classes, the Gothic Revival very quickly caught the fancy of many different groups and was soon popularized in commercial bottles, cast-iron stoves, and other mundane products. No doubt much of its popularity can be traced to Gothic novels of the day and to the widespread appeal of books on taste and architectural design. KSH

135 **Pepper Sauce Bottle**

Probably Boston, Massachusetts, area, ca. 1854 or later
Soda lime glass, paper
H. 8⅝ (21.92) W. 2 (5.08) D. 2 (5.08)
Collections of Greenfield Village and the Henry Ford Museum, Dearborn, Michigan
00.3.4562

In 1854 William K. Lewis and his brothers, C. P., E. J., and G. F. Lewis, were listed in Boston city directories as purveyors of "pickles, &c." One of their products, pepper sauce, came in a clear aquamarine glass bottle. It is clearly labeled, "SUPERIOR / PEPPER / SAUCE / W. K. LEWIS & BROS. / 93 / Broad Street / BOSTON." The Lewis brothers first worked at 93 Broad Street in 1854. KSH

136 Pickle Bottle

Probably Boston, Massachusetts, area, 1847 or later
Soda lime glass
H. 11½ (29.21) W. 3¾ (9.52) D. 3¾ (9.52)
Collections of Greenfield Village and the Henry Ford Museum, Dearborn, Michigan
28.206.9

In 1847 William Underwood owned a one-year-old spice-manufacturing concern and had just taken on two partners to form the firm of William Underwood and Company. Not long thereafter Underwood and Company must have ordered this bottle. Like the one later used by W. H. Davis (no. 137), the square Underwood pickle bottles were aquamarine with simple arched panels and a wide mouth. Underwood's bottles have been pressed in the mold with "WM. / UNDERWOOD / & C? / BOSTON." The William Underwood Company of Massachusetts survives today, although it has long since given up its distinctive packaging. KSH

137 Pickle Bottle

Probably Boston, Massachusetts, area, ca. 1851–1855
Soda lime glass, tin
H. 11¾ (29.85) W. 3½ (8.89) D. 3½ (8.89)
Collections of Greenfield Village and the Henry Ford Museum, Dearborn, Michigan
00.19.84

This tall, wide-necked, aquamarine bottle with long, boldly impressed arches and an embossed label may have been fabricated between 1851 and 1855. As late as the 1846–1847 Boston city directory, W. H. Davis is listed as a partner in William Underwood and Company (see no. 136), and it is not until 1851 that Davis appears independently as a manufacturer of "pickles &c." By 1860 he had taken on two partners and a second business address. Only from 1851 to 1855 did his directory listings correspond with the information on his label: "GHERKINS / WM. H. DAVIS / WHOLESALE / WAREHOUSE FOR / PICKLES / PRESERVES / SAUCES / &C / 37 BROAD ST. / BOSTON." KSH

138 Pickle Bottle

Probably United States, ca. 1850–1860
Soda lime glass
H. 14⅛ (35.88) DIAM. 4⅞ (12.39)
The Bayou Bend Collection, The Museum of Fine Arts, Houston, Texas B. 75.31

139 Pickle Bottle

Probably United States, ca. 1850–1860
Soda lime glass
H. 11³⁄₁₆ (28.42) W. 3⅝ (9.21) D. 3½ (8.89)
The Bayou Bend Collection, The Museum of Fine Arts, Houston, Texas B. 75.30

Common, clear, green glass pickle bottles came in a multitude of sizes and shapes. Of the two examples shown, the one on the right stands on a square base with side panels decorated in rather fine ogee arches, while the one on the left has a hexagonal base with arches on each panel. One of its panels conveniently lacks the diamond design to better accommodate a label. KSH

140 Vase

Attributed to the William Ellis Tucker Factory Philadelphia, Pennsylvania, ca. 1826–1838
Porcelain
H. 5⅞ (15.01) DIAM. 5¾ (14.61)
Collections of Greenfield Village and the Henry Ford Museum, Dearborn, Michigan
61.27.5

The design of this expanding vertical vase is the perfect vehicle for its polychrome flowers framed by thin cluster columns and wide, free-drawn, flamboyant arches. The latticework above each column suggests a simplistic two-dimensional representation of fan vaulting. Despite the medieval architectural detail the base itself is similar to beakers imported in the China trade. KSH

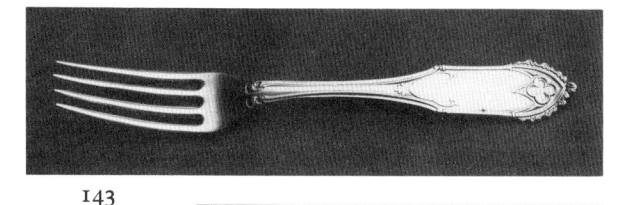

141   Covered Jar

     Attributed to Lyman, Fenton and Company
     Bennington, Vermont, ca. 1847–1858
     Glazed earthenware
     H. 9½ (24.13) DIAM. 8 (20.32)
     Collections of Greenfield Village and the Henry
       Ford Museum, Dearborn, Michigan
                                          00.6.165

Beginning in about 1835 Rockingham ware, or brown, mottled, glazed earthenware, was used in a large number of American homes. Popular forms included bowls, spittoons, clock cases, pitchers, urns, basins, and Gothic Revival covered jars, such as this one, probably made by Lyman, Fenton and Company of Bennington. The company also used the name United States Pottery Company from 1853 to 1858, when an advertisement of their Crystal Palace Exhibition included a similar covered jar.[1] A seemingly identical 11½-inch jar is labeled "Lyman Fenton & Co / Fenton's / ENAMEL / PATENTED / 1849 / Bennington, Vt."[2]   KSH

    1. Richard Carter Barret, *Bennington Pottery and Porcelain: A Guide to Identification*, 10, 14–15.
    2. *Ibid.*, 94.

142   Apostles Pitcher

     American Pottery Manufacturing Company,
       design attributed to Daniel Greatbach
     Jersey City, New Jersey, 1839–1852
     Glazed earthenware
     H. 9¼ (23.50) DIAM. 5⅜ (13.65)
     The Brooklyn Museum, Brooklyn, New York,
       Gift of Arthur W. Clement   43.128.27

In 1828 David Henderson acquired the defunct Jersey Porcelain and Earthenware Company and began a firm that would become well known for sophisticated "English style" stone and earthenware. Under the name American Pottery Manufacturing Company, which may have been abbreviated on its products to American Pottery Company, the firm hired Staffordshire potter Daniel Greatbach in 1839.[1] It is to Greatbach that this design is attributed. With eight draped apostles standing in elaborate niches and ornate pendant arches framing the spout, the pitcher illustrates the use of ornate Gothic Revival decorative devices on a rather common medium. Greatbach left Jersey City in 1852 and joined the United States Pottery Company in Bennington, Vermont, where he is credited with another apostles piece, a Rockingham water cooler.[2] The pitcher is marked on the bottom "AMERICAN / POTTERY Cº / JERSEY CITY,N.J."   KSH

    1. Lura Woodside Watkins, "Henderson of Jersey City and His Pitchers," *Antiques* L (December 1946), 388–392.
    2. *19th-Century America: Furniture and Other Decorative Arts*, no. 108.

143   Flatware: One Dinner Fork, Two Serving Spoons†, One Ladle†

     Gale and Hughes, and William Gale and Son
       (active partnerships ca. 1845–1860)
     New York, New York, ca. 1847–1855
     Silver
     Fork: L. 8 (20.32) W. 1 (2.54)
     Mr. Stephen R. Parks, New Haven, Connecticut

This fork is one example of a pattern of flatware made by several partnerships of William Gale (1799–1867)[1] from 1847, when the design was patented, on into the mid-1850s. Other examples in the same collection include serving spoons and a ladle with various dates between 1847 and 1855 and made by the partnership of Gale and Hughes as well as by William Gale and Son. Lancet windows, quatrefoils, crockets, and finials ornament both sides of the upturned handle terminal, and similar detail is applied at the base of the handle on the reverse side. DBW

1. *New York State Silversmiths* (Eggertsville, N.Y.: Darling Foundation of New York State Early American Silversmiths and Silver, 1964), 82.

† Not illustrated.

144 Tea† and Coffee† Pots, Waste Bowl

Andrew Ellicott Warner (1786–1870)
Baltimore, Maryland, ca. 1835–1850
Silver
Tea Pot: H. 14⅛ (35.88) W. 9¾ (24.77) DIAM. (at base) 4½ (11.43)
Coffee Pot: H. 15¾ (39.91) W. 10½ (26.67) DIAM. (at base) 5 (12.7)
Waste Bowl: H. 7¹⁵⁄₁₆ (20.17) DIAM. (at lip) 7¼ (18.42)
The Bayou Bend Collection, The Museum of Fine Arts, Houston, Texas
B. 69.525.1, 2, 4

Mid-nineteenth-century romantic taste often made little differentiation between historical styles, drawing freely on many and mixing them with a non-archeological eccleticism that resulted in a statement typical of that era. Here primarily Rococo ornament —flowers, leaves, scrolls, and phoenix birds—has been overlaid on neoclassical shapes. Mixed with the Rococo fantasy are exotic buildings—Chinese pagodas, Gothic churches, and buttressed and crenelated towers with Gothic windows. Andrew Ellicott Warner clearly marked each piece "A. E. WARNER" (serrated rectangle) and "11²" (rectangle with nipped corners), the latter indicating that the pieces are 92.5 percent silver. DBW

† Not illustrated.

145 Teapot

Sold by John and James Cox (active 1817–1853)
New York, New York, ca. 1835–1853
Silver
H. 8⅛ (20.65) W. 6⁹⁄₁₆ (16.61)
Private Collection

Examples of American hollowware in the Gothic Revival style are exceedingly rare. This small octagonal teapot recalls medieval Italian baptistries. Crenelations around the outer upper rim carry further medieval and architectural connotations. On six sides, engraved Gothic arches enclose bucholic scenes with rivers, bridges, and castles, all of which coincide with the romantic taste that shaped silver ornamentation in the 1830s and 1840s. The pot bears the mark of John and James Cox, who are generally known as retailers rather than as manufacturers. A pseudohallmark consisting of a star, anchor, and the letter "M," to date unidentified, may indicate the maker.[1] DBW

1. *New York State Silversmiths* (Eggertsville, N.Y.: Darling Foundation of New York State Early American Silversmiths and Silver, 1964), 60; and Ernest M. Currier, *Marks of Early American Silversmiths* (Harrison, N.Y.: Robert Alan Green, 1970), 36.

146 Shirred Rug

United States, ca. 1825–1860
Wool on linen backing
H. 40 (101.60) W. 72 (182.88)
Collections of Greenfield Village and the Henry Ford Museum, Dearborn, Michigan
30.157.2

From the mid-1820s until about 1860, the making of shirred rugs was a popular way to extend the life of fabric scraps. Strips of fabric were folded lengthwise and basted along the long edge. The basting thread was tightened to create a "caterpillar" that was then sewn to the backing.[1] In this instance the result was a blurred vision of a land far removed from a thrifty nineteenth-century American home. Perhaps borrowed from a print or book illustration, the design of this rug conjures up Gothic visions from Tennyson or Sir Walter Scott. KSH

1. Joel Kopp and Kate Kopp, *Hooked Rugs in the Folk Art Tradition*, [5].

145

145a

146

147 Ingrain Carpet Sample

　　　Possibly United States, 1840–1870
　　　Wool
　　　H. 21¾ (55.25) W. 21¾ (55.25)
　　　Reproduced through the Courtesy of the New York State Historical Association, Cooperstown, New York　　　N-550.61

As Americans grew more affluent and as ornate Victorian decor became increasingly elaborate, use of milled carpets woven in strips and laid "wall-to-wall" on the floors became required decor. This sample of ingrain carpet has no nap. It relies exclusively on a pattern of Gothic quatrefoils and rosettes to achieve a sense of visual appeal.　　　KSH

148 Window Shade

　　　United States, ca. 1850
　　　Printed cotton
　　　H. 31 (78.74) W. 48 (122.42)
　　　Society for the Preservation of New England Antiquities, Boston, Massachusetts
　　　　　　　　　　　　　　　　　　1945.151

Clover-like quatrefoils decorate the field of this shade while parallel rows of whimsical arches line each side. It is printed in three tones of brown on white. This example is the bottom part of a larger shade that was shortened at an undetermined earlier date.　　　KSH

149 Window Shade*

　　　Probably United States, ca. 1830–1849
　　　Cotton
　　　H. 60 (152.40) W. 31 (78.74)
　　　Essex Institute, Salem, Massachusetts
　　　　　　　　　　　　　　　　　107,128

With double-ended trefoil arches, shields within rosettes, and a repeat border of architecturally correct arches, this window shade relates very closely to another textile (no. 151) and to a wallpaper sample (no. 152), each used in mid-nineteenth-century Massachusetts. It is printed in shades of brown and green on a pale base fabric.　　　KSH

150 Pair of Window Shades

　　　Possibly New York, ca. 1830–1840
　　　Oil paint on Holland cloth
　　　H. 66 (167.64) W. 34 (86.36)
　　　Mr. William J. Jedlick

Window shades were frequently local products.[1] Hand-painted shades were decorated preferably in oil-base paints so that they might be cleaned with water. These two examples show Romanesque and Gothic castles set in rustic landscapes and were found in Albany, New York, in the Hudson River Valley. The romantic revival was an especially strong movement along the Hudson. Consequently, the scenes depicted here are most appropriate. These shades may illustrate romantic castles in New York State, but more likely they bear images derived from European prints. They brought gay colors and fashionable decoration to homes where people might cover their windows, but not their walls, with paintings.　　　KSH

1. As an example, William S. Segar (1823–1887) began his career as a window-shade painter in Utica, New York (George C. Groce and David H. Wallace, *The New-York Historical Society's Dictionary of Artists in America, 1564–1860*, p. 568). See also, William J. Jedlick, "Landscape Window Shades of the 19th Century in New York State and New England," (Master's thesis, State University of New York, College at Oneonta, 1967).

151 Fabric

　　　Possibly United States, ca. 1830–1835
　　　Cotton
　　　DIAM. 21½ (52.59)
　　　Essex Institute, Salem, Massachusetts
　　　　　　　　　　　　　　　　　104,591

This piece of fabric was once a stool cover. Its repeat pattern of arches, rosettes, and honeycombs is not unlike the cast-iron designs on Dr. Nott's base-burning stoves (no. 155). With brown, red, pink, yellow, blue, and green dyes on a white field, this fabric and others like it seem to have been popular on both sides of the Atlantic.[1]　　　KSH

1. For similar, but not identical textiles, see Florence M. Montgomery, *Printed Textiles: English and American Cottons and Linens, 1700–1850* (New York: Viking Press, 1970), 333–335; and 'Gothick,' 51.

152 Wallpaper

　　　United States, ca. 1840–1850
　　　Ink on paper
　　　H. 40½, 18¼ repeat (102.72, 46.36 repeat) W. 19 (48.26)
　　　Society for the Preservation of New England Antiquities, Boston, Massachusetts
　　　　　　　　　　　　　　　　　1911.101

In thirteenth-century France and England an architectural montage of this complexity would be found only on the superstructure of a great cathedral. In nineteenth-century America the design, deprived of its function and reduced to miniature, was applied to household walls. Purists such as Augustus Welby Northmore Pugin took issue with this sort of paper, preferring flat patterns with some prototypic basis to a confection of knights and arches.[1] However Pugin's wants and popular taste did not coincide. This particular wallpaper came from the Samuel P. Fowler House, built circa 1810, in Danversport, Massachusetts. It is printed in three shades of dark to medium brown on white.　　　KSH

1. Catherine Lynn Frangiamore, "Wallpapers Used in Nineteenth-Century America," *Antiques* CII (December 1972), 1044.

147

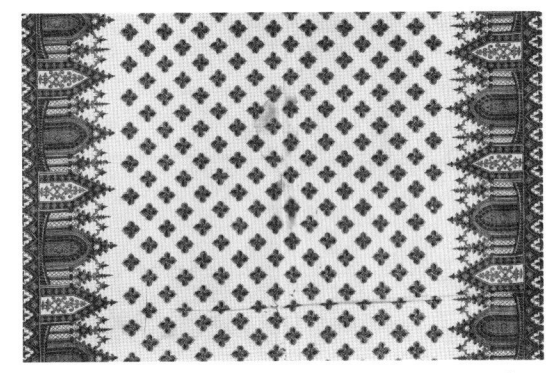

148

149

150    150

151

152

153   Wallpaper

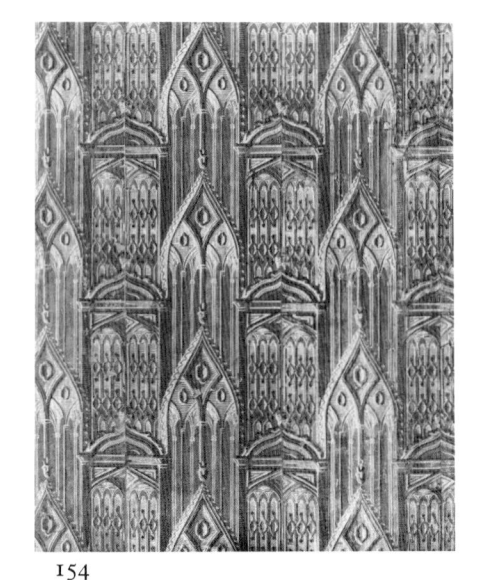

      Possibly United States, ca. 1850–1860
      Ink on paper
      H. 23 5/8 (60) W. 16 5/16 (41.5)
      Cooper-Hewitt Museum of Design, Smithsonian Institution, New York, New York
                            1938.62.7

"In selecting papers for cottages and for small dwellings, good taste will lead us to reject all showy and striking patterns, however beautiful in themselves —because they are out of keeping with the modest character of the cottage. Simple patterns—and those, if possible, which have some architectural expression accordant with that of the cottage—are most satisfactory."[1] Surely this pattern would appeal to Andrew Jackson Downing, because castles are brought indoors and combined with flat random foliage in a manner popular in midcentury America. Printed from a roller in colors of mauve-gray, green, and deep burgundy red on ivory, the paper would have been most appropriate in a Gothic Revival home of "modest character."   KSH

    1. Andrew Jackson Downing, *The Architecture of Country Houses*, 370n.

154   Wallpaper Sample

      Possibly United States, ca. 1840–1850
      Ink on paper
      H. 36 (91.44) W. 33 (83.82)
      C. R. and Susan C. Jones, Cooperstown, New York

With casual abandon the design of this wallpaper juxtaposes rows of middle and late Gothic windows in a manner that would have been unacceptable to the more scholarly medievalists who dominated Gothic Revival trends later in the century. Shades of brown and white conform to the taste for drab palettes popular in the 1840s. The paper appears to be roller printed on continuous roll paper. This sample was recovered from paneling removed from an unidentified New England home. Underneath was an earlier paper dating from circa 1820.   KSH

155 Base-Burning Stove

Shepard and Company (active ca. 1842–1848)
New York, New York, ca. 1842–1848
Cast iron
H. (including finials) 90 (228.60) W. (at base) 21 (53.34) D. (at base) 18 3/8 (46.67)
Philadelphia Museum of Art, Philadelphia, Pennsylvania, given by J. Kisterbock and Son, 1907   07-181

The gas light companies were mobbed,
The bakers all were shot,
The penny press began to talk
Of lynching Dr. Nott;
And all about the warehouse steps
Were angry men in droves,
Crashing and splintering through the doors
To smash the patent stoves.[1]

Prior to the War of 1812 America's primary heating fuels were native woods and soft, inefficient, bituminous coal imported from Great Britain. Our own abundant supply of hard, anthracite coal was not marketed because there were no stoves efficient enough to burn it. Dr. Eliphalet Nott (1773–1866), minister, philosopher, expert in "caloric," and president of Union College, changed all this when he patented the "Saracenic Stove" in 1826 and 1832. Nott simply introduced a rotary grate into stoves through which ashes could fall, allowing ample air to reach the unburned coals. Although Nott established "H. Nott and Company" to market his invention, he was almost immediately competing with other licensed and unlicensed makers who sold "Nott's Patent" stoves under their own labels.[2] The boxy stoves were ornamented with amusing blends of neoclassic and Gothic Revival modes. Standing on hairy paw feet, the unit here incorporates low-relief latticework arches, classical urns framed by arches, applied pilasters, rosettes, and the quintessence of classicism: a cast-iron rendering of Jacques Louis David's *Napoleon on Mont Saint-Bernard*.

Cast on the plate at the top center front of the stove is the label, "SHEPARD & CO / 242 / WATER ST N.Y." The words "NOTT'S PATENT" appear above the plate and above the burner. Shepard and Company first appears in New York city directories in 1842 as dealers in "Nott's stoves." By 1849 the company had dissolved.   KSH

1. Oliver Wendell Holmes, "The Hot Season" (1836), as quoted in Codman Hislop, *Eliphalet Nott* (Middletown, Conn.: Wesleyan University Press), 271.
2. Hislop, *Eliphalet Nott*, 255–271.

156 Box Stove

United States, ca. 1830–1838
Cast iron
H. 18 (45.72) W. 18 (45.72) D. 31 3/4 (80.65)
Collections of Greenfield Village and the Henry Ford Museum, Dearborn, Michigan
32.1623

Although much simpler than more exotic parlor stoves, this six-plate box stove is adorned with lancet arches and crockets. By tradition it belonged to Vermont governor Isaac Tichenor (1754–1838) and descended in his family.   KSH

157 Parlor Stove

George W. Eddy (active 1853–1875)
Troy, New York, ca. 1853
Cast iron
H. 40 (101.60) W. 32 (81.28) D. 17 (43.18)
Collections of Greenfield Village and the Henry Ford Museum, Dearborn, Michigan 24.46

According to city directories, George W. Eddy, maker of stoves and railroad car wheels, was one of the many iron founders who proliferated along River Street in Troy, New York. Eddy first appeared in Troy the year before he made the model for this stove. Cast on its base is "G. W. EDDY / TROY NY" and on either side of the tower "PAT'D 1853." Eddy continued making stoves until 1875.[1]   KSH

1. John G. Waite and Diana S. Waite, "Stovemakers of Troy, New York," *Antiques* CIII (January 1973), 144.

158 Parlor Stove*

Vose and Company (active 1848–1861)
Albany, New York, ca. 1854
Cast iron
H. 27 (68.58) W. 28 1/2 (72.39) D. 19 1/2 (49.53)
Collections of Greenfield Village and the Henry Ford Museum, Dearborn, Michigan
32.837.2

"Whoever loves symmetry and the simpler kind of cottage beauty, including good proportion, tasteful forms, and chasteness of ornament, we think, cannot but like this little design since it unites all of those requisites," wrote Andrew Jackson Downing about a small symmetrical cottage that he designed.[1] If Downing endorsed such a personification of beauty for one's home, why not move it indoors in the form of a cast-iron stove? This is exactly what Vose and Company did with their example labeled in cast, raised letters on the ashtray cover, "TEMPLE PARLOR NO. 4 / PATENTED 1854 / VOSE & CO. ALBANY N.Y."[2] Except for the exaggerated chimney on top and the feet, this stove personifies any number of Gothic Revival cottages and is very similar to the one Downing described in his book.   KSH

1. Andrew Jackson Downing, *The Architecture of Country Houses*, 104–108, quotation on page 104; see also, Z. Baker, *Modern House Builder, from the Log Cabin and Cottage to the Mansion*, 145.
2. This is just one of several Gothic Revival stoves manufactured by Vose and Company (see *Illustrated Book of Stoves Manufactured by Vose & Co., Albany, N.Y.* [Albany: Printed by E. H. Bender, 1854], pls. XXIII–XV).

158

159   160

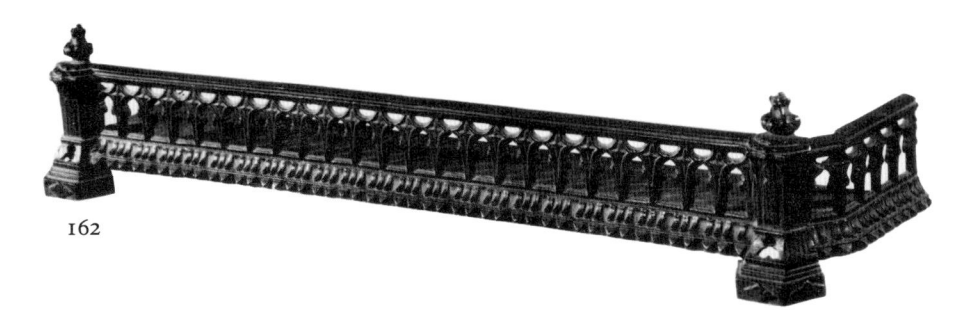

161

162

159 Mantel
Possibly Virginia, ca. 1850
Cast iron, paint
H. 49 (124.46) W. 65 (155.10) D. 9 (22.86)
Anne and David Sellin

Low, expansive Tudor arches formed attractive and functional frames to mid-nineteenth-century hearths. This particular Tudor mantel is one of a pair. It is painted with a marbling effect in slate gray while its mate is marbleized in maroon. The mantel is said to have been cast on the Samuel Finney-Hunter Johnson Plantation in Buchanan, Virginia. The plantation house was built in 1810, remodeled in mid-century, and survived until 1966, when it was demolished for a highway. KSH

160 Fireplace Inset
Probably United States, ca. 1840–1850
Cast iron
H. 32¾ (83.19) W. 33½ (85.09) D. 5 (12.70)
Anne and David Sellin

Fireplace insets radiated heat more evenly than did the standard exposed hearth. Here, the oriel (a cantilevered window adapted from medieval buildings), clustered columns, and Tudor arch frame bring the Gothic Revival style to that most sacred of nineteenth-century sites, the hearth. This inset came from a Washington, D.C., row house. KSH

161 Andirons or Fire Dogs
Savery and Company (ca. 1839–1869)
Philadelphia, Pennsylvania, ca. 1860–1869
Cast iron
H. 23¾ (60.33) W. 10¾ (27.31) D. 16½ (41.91)
Collections of Greenfield Village and the Henry Ford Museum, Dearborn, Michigan
30.969.1 A–B

Andirons are ideal vehicles for the Gothic Revival style. Their shafts are perfectly suited for tall, crocketed points, and their feet adapt easily to the Revival's ever-popular hexagonal columns. These particular examples are labeled in cast, raised letters, "SAVERY & CO. PHILADA / PATENTED APRIL 2D 1860." As early as 1845 Savery and

Company ran a half-page advertisement, noting that they were involved in the "Manufacture of all kinds of Iron Hollow-Ware, &c. SUCH AS Pots, Spiders, Bake Ovens, Kettles, . . . Stove Ware, Fire Dogs, . . . etc."[1] In 1869 the company changed its name to Barrow, Savery Company, thereby providing a probable terminal date for the years the andirons were manufactured.   KSH

1. John G. O'Brien, *O'Brien's Philadelphia Wholesale Business Directory* (Philadelphia: John G. O'Brien, 1845), 136.

162 Fireplace Fender

Probably United States, ca. 1840–1860
Cast iron
H. 5 13/16 (14.76) W. 41 (104.14) D. 10 3/8 (26.39)
Collections of Greenfield Village and the Henry Ford Museum, Dearborn, Michigan
30.969.4

For Gothic Revival cottages with cast-iron "Gothic" andirons and fireplaces framed in Tudor arches, what could be more appropriate than a medieval fender on the hearth?[1] The fender here, like so many other Gothic Revival objects, is decorated with a gallery of arches that serve a purely ornamental purpose. The medieval structural innovation was, in effect, reduced to a decorative device.   KSH

1. For a similar example, see David Henry Arnot, *Gothic Architecture to Modern Residences*, pl. 36.

163 Foot Scraper

Probably New York or New England, ca. 1845–1855
Cast iron
H. 13 (33.02) W. 17 (43.18) D. 13 (33.02)
Mr. Lee B. Anderson

According to family tradition, while honeymooning in the Hudson River Valley in the early 1840s, William J. Rotch (1819–1893) was so impressed by a Gothic villa that shortly thereafter he built his own Gothic house at 7 Orchard Street, New Bedford, Massachusetts.[1] That house was later described by Andrew Jackson Downing as "A Cottage-Villa In The Rural Gothic Style."[2] This small cast-iron foot scraper was made for the house and descended in the family until purchased by the present owner.   DBW

1. John M. Bullard, *The Rotches* (New Bedford, Mass.: By the Author, 1947), 105. The house, built circa 1845, is still standing. Rotch, a successful manufacturer of textiles, was New Bedford's leading citizen during much of the nineteenth century.
2. Andrew Jackson Downing, *The Architecture of Country Houses*, 295–298, caption on page 295.

164 Birdhouse

Miller Iron Company (begun ca. 1866, still active 1892)
Providence, Rhode Island, ca. 1868
Cast iron
H. 15 (38.10) DIAM. 9 (22.86)
Mr. Lee B. Anderson

165 Birdhouse

Miller Iron Company
Providence, Rhode Island, ca. 1868
Cast iron
H. 12 (30.48) W. 14 1/2 (36.83) D. 12 (30.48)
Mr. Lee B. Anderson

In western Rhode Island a number of Gothic Revival houses survive today, some equipped with cast-iron birdhouses, such as these examples. The houses pictured here were both made by the firm of William H. Miller, general blacksmiths, machine and tool forgers, and each bears the inscription "MILLER IRON CO., PROVIDENCE, R.I. APRIL 14, 1868." The Miller Company began in 1866 under the title of Crowell and Miller, later became Miller and Sisson, and eventually came under sole control of William H. Miller. The business was located at 194, 196, and 200 Eddy Street. While Miller's octagonal birdhouse with bird finial is somewhat fanciful, the other example follows closely the design of Gothic Revival villas and cottages.   DBW

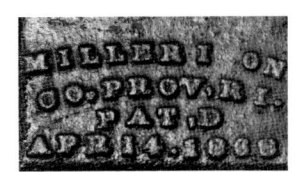

163

164

165

165a

166 *Mediterranean Coast Scene with Tower*
Thomas Cole (1801–1848)
New York, after 1832
Oil on panel
H. 26¾ (67.95) W. 34 (86.36)
Collection of the Albany Institute of History
and Art, Albany, New York   1965.1

Sometime during Thomas Cole's years in Italy (1831–1832), he sketched one or more crumbling towers along the Italian coast (no. 181). When he returned to the United States he developed his sketches repeatedly and did so with far more dramatic feeling than is expressed in his earlier work. In part Cole introduced a temporal quality to his art. No longer did he paint virgin New York landscapes seen for the first time. This painting and others like it show nature as an infinite element continuing unabated as man's civilizations rise and decay.[1]

The painting illustrated here, which is signed "T. Cole" in the lower center, may have been the one that Cole titled *Solitude* and consigned to George Cook for sale in 1844. *Solitude* was returned to Cole's widow unsold in 1848. The *Mediterranean Coast Scene* remained in the Cole family until it was purchased by its present owner in 1964.[2]   KSH

1. Louis Legrand Noble, *The Life and Works of Thomas Cole*, edited by Elliot S. Vesell (1853; reprint, Cambridge, Mass.: Harvard University Press, Belknap Press, 1964), 110.
2. Howard S. Merritt, *Thomas Cole*, no. 26.

167 *The Departure**

Thomas Cole (1801–1848)
New York, 1837
Oil on canvas
H. 39½ (100.33) W. 63 (160.02)
In the Collection of the Corcoran Gallery of Art, Washington, D.C.   69.2

168 *The Return**

Thomas Cole (1801–1848)
New York, 1837
H. 39¾ (100.97) W. 63 (160.02)
In the Collection of the Corcoran Gallery of Art, Washington, D.C.   69.3

In 1837 William P. van Rensselaer commissioned Thomas Cole to paint *The Departure* and *The Return*.[1] Both paintings are dated 1837 and both are signed; the former shows "TC" in the lower right center and the latter, "T Cole," also in the lower right center.[1] Cole described the paintings to van Rensselaer in the following manner: "The story . . . is taken neither from history nor poetry: it is a fiction of my own, if incidents which must have occurred very frequently can be called fiction. It is supposed to have date in the 13th or 14th century.

"In the first picture, Morning, which I call The Departure, a dark and lofty castle stands on an eminence, embosomed in woods. . . . In the foreground is a sculptured Madonna, by which passes a road, winding beneath ancient trees, and, crossing a stream by a Gothic bridge, conducting to the gate of the castle. . . . the Lord of the Castle, reins in his charger, and turns a look of pride and exhultation [*sic*] at the castle of his fathers and his gallant retinue. . . .

"The second picture—The Return—is in early autumn. The sun is low: its yellow beams gild the pinnacles of an abbey, standing in a shadowy wood. . . . the lord is borne on a litter, dead or dying—his charger led behind—a single knight, and one or two attendants—all that war has spared of that once goodly company."[2] To romantic poet William Cullen Bryant *The Departure* and *The Return* were among Cole's "noblest works."[3]

    KSH

1. *A Catalogue of the Collection of American Paintings in the Corcoran Gallery of Art, I: Painters Born before 1850* (2 vols., Washington, D.C.: Corcoran Gallery of Art, 1966–1973), 62.
2. Letter from Thomas Cole to William P. van Rensselaer, Catskill, New York, October 15, 1837, as published in Louis Legrand Noble, *The Life and Works of Thomas Cole*, edited by Elliot S. Vesell (1853; reprint, Cambridge, Mass.: Harvard University Press, Belknap Press, 1964), 181–182.
3. Noble, *Life and Works of Thomas Cole*, 182.

169

171

170

172

169 *Fanciful Landscape*

Thomas Doughty (1793–1856)
Boston, Massachusetts, 1834
Oil on canvas
H. 30⅛ (76.53) W. 39⅞ (100.86)
National Gallery of Art, Washington, D.C.,
  Gift of the Avalon Foundation 1963 1907

Fanciful Landscape is an early work by one of America's first landscape painters, Philadelphian Thomas Doughty. By 1821 Doughty had completed a night course in painting, had abandoned his trade as a leather currier, and had begun painting views of gentlemen's estates.[1] From 1826 to 1830 and again from 1832 to 1837 Doughty worked in Boston teaching painting and exhibiting both real and imagined landscapes. *Fanciful Landscape* was one of his Boston creations. Signed "T. DOUGHTY / Boston / 1834" in the lower right, it is similar in concept to another of his works, *Romantic Landscape with Temple*, also done during his Boston years.[2] Although both works were painted before Doughty ever journeyed to Europe, they reflect a compositional concept remarkably similar to that used by Claude Lorrain in the seventeenth century.[3] Both Claude and Doughty use hazy distances and a brilliant, low sun to establish alternating planes in light and shade; and both turn to benign pastoral scenes as objects of their attention. Few scenes could be more removed from eastern Massachusetts or better suited to the romantic mind than this castle on a cliff.   KSH

1. M. and M. Karolik Collection of American Paintings: 1815 to 1865 (Cambridge, Mass.: Museum of Fine Arts, Boston, 1949), 218.
2. *Romantic Landscape with Temple* is owned by the Smith College Museum of Art, Northampton, Massachusetts.
3. Thomas N. Maytham, "A Trove of Doughtys," *Antiques* LXXXVIII (November 1965), 681–685.

170 *Sunnyside*

George Inness (1825–1894)
New York, ca. 1847–1849
Oil on canvas
H. 14¾ (37.47) W. 19¾ (50.17)
Sleepy Hollow Restorations, Tarrytown, New
  York

Sunnyside, the home of Washington Irving, stood not far down the Hudson River from Newburgh, New York, the community where George Inness was born.[1] Since Sunnyside began its life as a seventeenth-century Dutch farmhouse, which Irving did not remodel until 1835–1839, both Inness and Sunnyside entered their romantic phases at the same time. Inness probably painted this small canvas before his extended European visit from 1850 to 1852.[2] His overgrown, remote interpretation of Sunnyside, situated up an isolated winding lane, provides a scene equal to one of Irving's best tales, "The Legend of Sleepy Hollow." The painting also illustrates a difference in perception between Inness and artists of the Hudson River School. Here Inness paints a microcosm of the grandiose scenes done by Thomas Cole and Frederic Church. The painting precedes Inness's later interest in the French Barbizon school of painting.   KSH

1. George C. Groce and David H. Wallace, *The New-York Historical Society's Dictionary of Artists in America, 1564–1860*, pp. 340–341.
2. LeRoy Ireland, *The Works of George Inness: An Illustrated* Catalogue Raisonné, xix–xx, 17.

171 *Fight below the Battlements**

Thomas Worthington Whittredge (1820–1910)
Düsseldorf, Germany, 1849
Oil on canvas
H. 25 (63.50) W. 33½ (85.09)
Vose Galleries, Boston, Massachusetts

With a delightful touch of humor, Whittredge has pitted in mortal combat American frontiersmen against European Defenders of the Faith at the base of a fourteenth-century fortress. Surely this is one of the most unusual adaptations of Europe's Gothic style to American taste seen thus far. Whittredge spent his childhood in Ohio and was trained as a house and sign painter, a daguerreotype maker, and a portraitist. In 1843 he began to paint landscapes, and just three years later his first work in this genre was accepted by the National Academy of Design. Armed with several commissions for European landscapes, Whittredge departed for a ten-year stay abroad in 1849, settling first in Düsseldorf, where he painted and signed this work, "T.W. Whittridge / Dusseldorf 1849."[1] An entry in Whittredge's journal and account book for April 15, 1850, reads: "Castle of Drachenfels, storm with a skirmish of knights. For Davis B. Lawler. Price $100, commissioned May 5, 1849."[2] *Fight below the Battlements*, which may be the painting in question, is no doubt an amalgam of his American past and his new European experiences.   KSH

1. This artist variously signed his name Whitridge, Whittridge, and Whittredge, assuming the last about 1858. By 1855 Whittredge had ceased to use his forename in his signature (Edward H. Dwight, "Worthington Whittredge, Artist of the Hudson River School," *Antiques* XCVI [October 1969], 582).
2. This information appears on page 126 of Whittredges' journal and account book and was kindly provided by Mr. Robert C. Vose, Jr.

172 *Mrs. Abbott Lawrence*

Chester Harding (1792–1866)
Boston, Massachusetts, 1840–1850
Oil on canvas
H. 27½ (69.80) W. 22¼ (56.50)
Museum of Fine Arts, Boston, Massachusetts,
  Gift of Misses Aimee and Rosamond Lamb
    61.240

"When I was painting portraits in Utica," wrote William Dunlap, upon meeting Chester Harding, "I was pleased with his appearance and manners, I noticed that he immediately selected the best head I had painted there—proof of a true eye and taste. I again met him in Boston, and witnessed the impression his talents made in that city previous to his going to Europe."[1] Although born in New Hampshire, Harding was one of many Americans who moved west in the early decades of the nineteenth century. After trying his hand at chair making and sign painting he discovered his natural ability to paint portraits and returned to New England. Harding, the country lad, became the darling of Boston and a popular successor to Gilbert Stuart. Sometime during the 1840s he painted the portraits of Mr. and Mrs. Abbott Lawrence.[2] Mrs. Lawrence, a graceful but not very pretty woman, is seated on a painted Gothic Revival side chair with flowered upholstery. No chair quite like this one has been discovered: its silhouette is very simple, but what the chair lacks in complexity of form it augments with an elaborate upholstery, braid, and a painted frame. Half-hidden behind a delightfully rendered knitting basket is a brass cap on the rear leg of the chair. Although casters are frequently seen on

Gothic chairs, the cap is but another special touch on this singular chair.   KSH

1. William Dunlap, *History of the Rise and Progress of the Arts of Design in the United States*, II, 295.
2. *19th-Century America: Paintings and Sculpture*, no. 38.

173 Mr. and Mrs. Charles Henry Augustus Carter

Probably Nicholas Biddle Kittell (1822–1894)
Probably New York, ca. 1848
Oil on canvas
H. 24 (60.96) W. 22¼ (56.52)
Museum of the City of New York, Gift of Mrs. Edward C. Moen   62.234.12

"If hospitality smiles in ample parlors; if home virtues dwell in cosy, fireplace family-rooms; if the love of the beautiful is seen in picture or statue galleries; intellectuality, in well-stocked libraries; and even a dignified love of leisure and repose, in cool and spacious verandas; we feel, at a glance, that here we have reached the highest beauty of which Domestic Architecture is capable—that of individual expression."[1] In midcentury America, where a prosperous middle class was springing from agricultural backgrounds, appearances were important. Throughout Andrew Jackson Downing's writings and those of his contemporaries, there is a recurrent theme that if one looked genteel and lived in a genteel manner, one became genteel by association if not by birth. This portrait depicts a refined couple, Mr. and Mrs. Charles Henry Augustus Carter, seated in their living room at 11 Bleecker Street, New York. They espouse all of those domestic virtues so admired in the nineteenth century. Mr. Carter, who was assistant superintendent of New York Hospital in 1843–1844, could afford many amenities including contemporary living-room furnishings in Restauration and Gothic styles. This painting shows that there were very few purely Gothic homes like Roseland or Lyndhurst; like today, there were many happily mixed periods or revivals within traditional settings. The Carters were probably painted by Nicholas Biddle Kittell, a landscape and portrait painter whose initials "NBK" appear in the lower left corner of the canvas.   KSH

1. Andrew Jackson Downing, *Cottage Residences, Rural Architecture, and Landscape Gardening*, 23.

174 The Four Children of Marcus L. Ward

Lilly Martin Spencer (1822–1902)
Newark, New Jersey, ca. 1858
Oil on canvas
H. 92 (233.68) W. 68½ (173.99)
Collection of the Newark Museum, Newark, New Jersey   21.1913

Few artists so exemplified all the best domestic virtues in nineteenth-century America as Lilly Martin Spencer. Although born in France, Mrs. Spencer lived in Cincinnati until she, her tailor husband, and their two children moved to New York in 1848 and subsequently to Newark in 1857. As a middle-class wife and mother she seemed to bring the domesticity, realism, and warmth to her paintings so admired by the middle classes in this country and abroad. Evidently the Spencers were short of funds when they moved to Newark, for Mrs. Spencer agreed to do three paintings for Marcus Lawrence Ward in exchange for two years rent. Included was a full-length portrait with four figures, undoubtedly this group painting.[1] In it Joseph, Marcus Jr., Catherine, and Francis Ward are posed on a gigantic Gothic armchair with Rococo Revival legs. Although the location of the chair is not known and the numbers "1713" carved in the crest rail are an enigma, it recalls a talented cabinetmaker, John Jelliff (no. 38), who was working in Newark in the Gothic style at this time.
   KSH

1. Susan Solomon, "American Fine Arts in the Newark Museum, Part II: The Nineteenth Century," *Antiques* CIII (March 1973), 490; and Robin Bolton-Smith, "The Sentimental Paintings of Lilly Martin Spencer," *Antiques* CIV (July 1973), 108–115.

175 James Lithgow*

Possibly Louisville, Kentucky, ca. 1866
Oil on canvas
H. 50 (127.00) W. 41 (104.14)
The Filson Club, Louisville, Kentucky

James Smith Lithgow (1812–1902), tin and copper-smith, businessman, councilman, and mayor of Louisville, Kentucky, from 1866 to 1867 was painted sitting in a Gothic Revival armchair posed in front of a view of the Louisville City Hall. Mayor

Lithgow's chair is but another variation on popular arm and side chairs of the day (see nos. 27, 28, and 29). KSH

176 *First Reading of the Emancipation Proclamation**

Francis Bicknell Carpenter (1830–1900)
United States, 1864
Oil on canvas
H. 108 (279.40) W. 174 (457.20)
Architect of the Capitol, Washington, D.C.

On September 22, 1862, President Abraham Lincoln announced that "on the first day of January, A.D. 1863, all persons held as slaves within any state or designated part of a state the people whereof shall then be in rebellion against the United States shall be then, thenceforward, and forever free."[1] By 1864, although the Civil War was not over, Francis Bicknell Carpenter had interpreted this occasion as it was supposed to have occurred when Lincoln was reading the Emancipation Proclamation for the first time to (left to right) Edwin M. Stanton, Salmon P. Chase, Gideon Wells, Caleb B. Smith, William H. Seward, Montgomery Blair, and Edward Bates.[2]

In executing his most famous painting and recording an important historic event, the New York portrait painter also documented some fine White House chairs. The Restauration-style chairs with lancet arches and trefoils seen in the foreground may well be three of the twenty-four chairs bought by the White House from John and Joseph W. Meeks of New York in 1846 and 1847 (see nos. 4 and 5). The painting was popularized by mezzotint (no. 177) and subsequently was presented to the United States Capitol, where it now hangs in the west staircase of the Senate Wing. KSH

1. Henry Bamford Parks, *The United States of America: A History* (New York: Alfred A. Knopf, 1957), 365.
2. *Compilation of Works of Art and Other Objects in the United States Capitol* (Washington, D.C., 1965), 129.

177

178

179

180

181

84

177   *The First Reading of the Emancipation Proclamation before the Cabinet*

Francis Bicknell Carpenter, artist; Alexander Hay Ritchie, engraver
Probably New York, New York, after 1865
Mezzotint heightened by engraving on paper
H. 27 (68.58) W. 36 (78.74)
Western Reserve Historical Society, Cleveland, Ohio   347

Nineteenth-century academic painters such as Francis Carpenter were frequently entrepreneurs as well as artists. They enrolled subscribers for their works, exhibited for a fee, often auctioned paintings, and turned them over to printers for popular reproduction and distribution. Carpenter's *First Reading of the Emancipation Proclamation* (no. 176) was an appropriate subject for mass marketing. With neither illustrated newspapers nor television, the public was ripe for visual documentation of this historic event. Although Ritchie did adjust Carpenter's composition to a degree (note that the portrait on the door and the sword have been changed), possibly because he was converting a large polychromed composition to a small, monochromatic piece of paper, he clearly illustrates the lancet-back side chairs, which may have been purchased from John and Joseph W. Meeks in 1846–1847 (nos. 4 and 5).   KSH

178   *Hallock House. 1836.*

Probably New England, ca. 1836–1885
Oil on wood panel
H. 33 (83.8) W. 55¼ (140.3)
New Haven Colony Historical Society, New Haven, Connecticut   1971.63

By 1836 Gerard Hallock (1800–1866) was a prosperous newspaper man and part-owner of the *New York Journal of Commerce*. He was also the owner of a new castellated house designed by Sidney M. Stone, which occupied forty acres of land on New Haven's Oyster Point. Hallock continued to live in his castle until his death, at which time it was bought by the New York and New Haven Railroad. The railroad moved the house, turned it around, and enlarged it for occupancy by railroad officials. Hallock House survived until 1939 and was used as a multifamily dwelling before its demolition.

This charming panel, heavily framed and made of wood, has all the characteristics of an inn sign, although Hallock House never seems to have served such a public function. Perhaps the sign, until entering the present collection in 1885, marked the railroad's property.   KSH

179   *Fireboard*

Probably New England, ca. 1845
Oil on wood
H. 32½ (82.55) W. 40 (101.60)
Childs Gallery, Boston, Massachusetts

It is fairly common to find simple wood-framed Tudor-arch mantels ornamenting the hearths of modest Gothic cottages. This firescreen would have been an appropriate cover for a revivalist hearth. In a clever trompe l'oeil technique, a container of fruit and flowers sits on a gray marble pedestal that stands in a dark recess apparently framed by a mocha-brown arch.[1]   KSH

1. Nina Fletcher Little, *American Decorative Wall Painting, 1700–1850*, p. 140.

180   *Country Scene*

Jasper Francis Cropsey (1823–1900)
New Jersey, January 7, 1847
Pencil, pale brown wash, white gouache on paper
H. 8¼ (21.00) W. 11 9/16 (29.40)
Cooper-Hewitt Museum of Design, Smithsonian Institution, New York, New York   1948-127-2

Shortly before J. F. Cropsey left for a two-year honeymoon in Europe, he sketched this modest cottage, which probably stood somewhere near Greenwood Lake, Orange County, New Jersey. The house in the distance, the mountains behind it, and two ancient trees merging into one speak eloquently of the romantic atmosphere that could surround a Gothic cottage. Cropsey had exhibited at the National Academy of Design and knew Thomas Cole's romantic landscapes, but it was not until he went to England that he was truly introduced to the Gothic Revival: in the summer of 1847 he and his bride visited Sir Walter Scott's Abbotsford and other British castles and ruins before going on to Italy. Appropriately, Cropsey occasionally closed some of his correspondence with lines from Scott's *Marmion* and was described by Henry Tuckerman as having "a remarkable tact and truth in color and a true sense of the picturesque."[1] Cropsey repeatedly painted medieval ruins, including *The Isle of Capri* (1848) and *Corfe Castle and Town from the Cromwell Trenches* (circa 1857).[2]   KSH

1. Peter Birmingham, *Jasper F. Cropsey, 1823–1900: A Retrospective View of America's Painter of Autumn*, 7–8, 11, quotation on page 13.
2. William S. Talbot, "Jasper F. Cropsey, Child of the Hudson River School," *Antiques* XCII (November 1967), 713–717.

181   *Ruined Castle by a Bay*

Thomas Cole (1801–1848)
New York, ca. 1832[1]
Pencil highlighted with white on gray paper
H. 14 7/16 (36.6) W. 10⅛ (25.73)
Detroit Institute of Arts, Detroit, Michigan, William H. Murphy Fund   DIA 39.385

No rays from the holy heaven come down
On the long night-time of that town;
But light from out the lurid sea
Streams up the turrets silently—
Gleams up the pinnacles far and free—
Up domes—up spires—up kingly halls—
Up fanes—up Babylon-like walls—
Up shadowy long-forgotten bowers
Of sculptured ivy and stone flowers—
Up many and many a marvelous shrine
Whose wreathèd friezes intertwine
The viol, the violet, and the vine.[2]

Edgar Allan Poe's mythical castle is little different from Thomas Cole's shadowy ruin guarding a distant bay. The mystery and melancholy of a deserted tower seen on a cloudy day contribute to the romantic mood that permeated American nineteenth-century literature and art. Perhaps, too, the middle and upper middle classes who derived their prosperity from the Industrial Revolution for the first time identified themselves with the people who owned the castles and not with the serfs who worked within

182

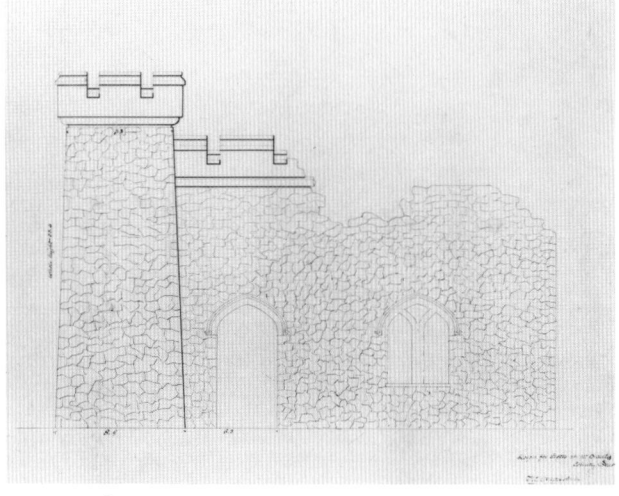

183

them. The image of a desolate castle occurs time and time again in Cole's works (no. 166). Most of them date from Cole's spring in Italy in 1832.[3]   KSH

1. Howard S. Merritt, *Thomas Cole*, 113.
2. Edgar Allan Poe, "The City in the Sea," in F. O. Matthiessen, ed., *The Oxford Book of American Verse* (New York: Oxford University Press, 1952), 208.
3. Merritt, *Thomas Cole*, 73, 76–77, 84–85.

182 Sandpaper Drawing

United States, ca. 1860
Charcoal on paper
H. 9¼ (23.50) W. 11¼ (28.58)
Reproduced through the Courtesy of the New York State Historical Association, Cooperstown, New York   N-47.50

Charcoal drawings on sandpaper were naive innovations of the nineteenth century. Not only did sandpaper hasten the application of charcoal to the surface, but the sand's reflective quality made it sparkle. Thus a practical medium was used to record a romantic subject: a ruined castle sits on a tiny island, dark clouds swirl around it, and boats move on a lake with a rushing waterfall. As with many naive works the end product is a whimsical interpretation of what would otherwise be an eerie scene.   KSH

183 *Design for Grotto at Mr. Biddles Country Seat*

Thomas Ustick Walter (1804–1887)
Philadelphia, Pennsylvania, 1834–1836
Ink on paper
Framed: H. 21 (53.34) W. 16½ (41.91)
Mr. and Mrs. James Biddle

In 1834 Philadelphia banker Nicholas Biddle commissioned T. U. Walter to "modernize" his Federal-style country house on the banks of the Delaware River. Biddle had worked with Walter on the Greek Revival designs for Girard College, and since he wanted Andalusia to be redone in the same style, he turned to Walter again. Evidently neither Biddle nor Walter found it strange to place a Gothic ruin on the grounds of an American Greek Revival house whose center section was fashioned in the spirit of an ancient Grecian temple, the Hephaestum.[1] The idea of combining different architectural modes on the same property was hardly new: Sanderson Miller designed the English Palladian country house Hagley Hall in Staffordshire in the mid-eighteenth century and installed a "Gothick" ruin not unlike Walter's on the property. About ten years after the improvement of Andalusia and the building of the grotto and a Greek Revival billiard room, Walter added a Gothic Revival cottage to the grounds, which was published in his *Cottage and Villa Architecture*.[2]   KSH

1. Harold Donaldson Eberlein and Cortlandt Van Dyke Hubbard, "Living with Antiques: Nicholas Biddle's Andalusia," *Antiques* LXIII (April 1952), 339–343; and James Biddle, "Nicholas Biddle's Andalusia, a Nineteenth Century Country Seat Today," *Antiques* LXXXV (September 1964), 286–290.
2. Thomas Ustick Walter and John Jay Smith, *Two Hundred Designs for Cottages and Villas*, pl. L.

184 *Otsego Hall*

John William Hill, artist; John H. Bufford, lithographer; Lewis P. Clover, publisher
New York, New York, 1837–1839
Lithograph on paper
H. 8½ (21.59) W. 12 (30.48)
Reproduced through the courtesy of the New York State Historical Association, Cooperstown, New York   N-335.63

In 1834, following an extended European visit, James Fenimore Cooper, author and anglophile, returned to his family home in Cooperstown, New York, and immediately began remodeling his Federal-style house. By foregoing a "Grecian abortion," he set the stage for his role as "Squire of Cooperstown."[1] Cooper described his home in the following way: "All is brick except the roof and window sills. The whole is a light gray produced by a wash of lime, sand and copperas. The entrance is into a small tower in which you ascend to your favorite hall. This room has undergone no material change with the exception of the ceiling being raised three feet. This change I believe is universally admitted to be an improvement. . . . All the lower rooms, including drawing-room, library, dining-room, and breakfast-parlor are to be as formerly, but the chambers are essentially altered being in the first place, raised from ten feet in hight [sic] to thirteen."[2] Otsego Hall remained Cooper's home un-

86

til his death in 1851. It then became a hotel, which subsequently burned in 1853.³

Cooper was at the height of his career when he remodeled Otsego Hall. His fame and the Hall's design, unusual for the 1830s, made it a likely subject for a lithograph. The lithograph carries the following legend: "From a Drawing by J.W. Hill / OTSEGO HALL / The residence of James Fenimore Cooper Esq. / Published by L.P. Clover, 294 Broadway / Buffords Lith.N.Y." It seems likely that Hill recorded Otsego Hall during his years as a landscape and topographical painter. This lithograph was probably produced between 1837 and 1839, the only years, according to New York city directories, when Lewis P. Clover sold looking glasses at 294 Broadway and John H. Bufford was working in New York.⁴ The noble savages in the foreground may well be two of Cooper's characters from his Leatherstocking Tales.

KSH

1. James Fenimore Cooper, *Home as Found* (2 vols., Philadelphia: Lea and Blanchard, 1838), I, p. 145.
2. James Fenimore Cooper to Micah Sterling, October 27, 1834, letter in the Collection of American Literature, Beinecke Rare Book and Manuscript Library, Yale University, New Haven, Connecticut.
3. For more information on Otsego Hall, see Katherine B. Susman, "Gothic Revival Domestic Architecture in Cooperstown, New York, 1834–1868: The Evolution of a Style" (Master's thesis, State University of New York, College at Oneonta, 1971), 13–28.
4. George C. Groce and David H. Wallace, *The New-York Historical Society's Dictionary of Artists in America, 1564–1860*, pp. 94, 316.

185 *The Harral-Wheeler House*
   Alexander Jackson Davis (1803–1892)
   New York, New York, ca. 1846–1847
   Ink and wash on paper
   H. 14³⁄₈ (36) w. 19⁵⁄₈ (50)
   Avery Architectural Library, Columbia University, New York, New York, A. J. Davis Collection   Z-2

"Mayor Harral is building an extensive Castle on the lot attached to his present residence on Golden Hill.—It will be of the Gothic order, fronting about 76 feet and extending back about 100 feet, and there are to be towers and *what nots*. The main tower will be some 60 feet in height.—The building, which is to be brick with stucco, will be completed by another summer. It will make a very handsome appearance." So wrote the *Republican Standard* about Mayor Henry Kollock Harral's (1808–1854) elaborate Gothic Revival villa in Bridgeport, Connecticut, designed by Alexander Jackson Davis and similar to Davis's earlier design of the Waddell House (no. 191) on the corner of Fifth Avenue and 37th Street in New York.¹

Henry Harral was a self-made man whose home may have been a monument to his own success. Certainly it rivaled the home of another Bridgeport entrepreneur, P. T. Barnum, whose Iranistan was an extraordinary villa in the oriental style. "Walnut Wood," as Harral's house came to be known, followed an irregular floor plan; Davis grouped rooms as common sense dictated without being bound by a need for symmetry. Both the exterior elevation of the house and the interior room arrangement reflect this irregularity. Evidently Davis was pleased with both the Harral House and this rendering; in all probability this is the drawing he exhibited at the 1853 New York World's Fair and again in 1865 at the National Academy of Design.² In 1866 the house was acquired by another manufacturer, Nathaniel Wheeler. Walnut Wood remained in the Wheeler family until 1956; two years later it was demolished.

KSH

1. *Republican Standard*, August 10, 1847, as quoted in Anne Castrodale Golovin, *Bridgeport's Gothic Ornament: The Harral-Wheeler House*, 5, 3.
2. The rendering bears a separate label reading: "English Collegiate Gothic Mansion of Mrs. Harral at Bridgeport, Ct. Alexr. J. Davis, Architect" (Golovin, *Bridgeport's Gothic Ornament*, 6).

186 *Roseland*
Attributed to Joseph C. Wells or his office
New York, New York, ca. 1846
Watercolor on paper
H. 12¾ (32.39) W. 17¾ (45.09)
Society for the Preservation of New England Antiquities, Boston, Massachusetts
1970.442

In 1845 Henry Chandler Bowen (1813–1896), successful New York merchant and publisher, commissioned New York architect Joseph Wells to design an appropriate country house to be built on a site in Woodstock, Connecticut, a small village in the northeastern part of the state.[1] Roseland or "The Pink House" is a Gothic Revival cottage both inside and out. It was completely furnished in the Gothic style at the time it was built, and these furnishings remain there today. Bowen seems to have been an appropriate owner for this house, for according to the sage of America's Gothic Revival, Andrew Jackson Downing, pointed cottages were for "men of imagination—men whose aspirations will never leave them at rest—men whose ambition and energy will give them no peace within the mere bounds of rationality. These are the men for picturesque villas—country houses with high roofs, steep gables, unsymmetrical and capricious forms." It was Downing, too, who described white exteriors as being "absolutely painful" and advocated *"soft and quiet shades"* such as pink with darker trim, noting "a certain sprightliness is therefore always bestowed on a dwelling in a neutral tint, by painting the bolder projecting features of a different shade."[2]

KSH

1. Ruth Davidson, "Roseland, a Gothic Revival Mansion," *Antiques* LXXXI (May 1962), 510–514.
2. Andrew Jackson Downing, *The Architecture of Country Houses*, 263, 198, 202, 204.

187 *Kenwood*
    Alexander Jackson Davis (1803–1892)
    New York, New York, ca. 1842
    Watercolor on paper
    H. 7$\frac{1}{12}$ (18) W. 10¼ (25.8)
    Avery Architectural Library, Columbia University, New York, New York, A. J. Davis Collection   15-1

"Two miles south of Albany, on a densely wooded hill, is the villa of Joel Rathbone, Esq., . . . one of the most complete specimens of the Tudor style in the United States. It was built from the designs of [Alexander Jackson] Davis, and is, to the amateur, a very instructive example of this mode of domestic architecture."[1] So wrote Andrew Jackson Downing about Davis's 1842 design for Kenwood, when he published a version of this drawing. Downing also commented quite favorably on the "Gallilee," the small anteroom "with a seat or two for servants waiting," where guests might shed their wraps prior to entering the hall.[2]

With a steeply pitched roof, long low veranda, tall clustered chimneys, and an irregular floor plan, Kenwood shares many of the same attributes that mark other Davis houses. The stepped gable above the carriageway is a pleasant romantic touch reminiscent of Washington Irving's Sunnyside (no. 170).
    KSH

1. Andrew Jackson Downing, *A Treatise on the Theory and Practice of Landscape Gardening, Adapted to North America, With a View to the Improvement of Country Residences*, 400n.
2. *Ibid.*, 400.

188 Four Sketches for Furniture at Lyndhurst
    Alexander Jackson Davis (1803–1892)
    New York, New York, 1841–1847
    Pencil on paper
    H. 4⅜ (11) W. 6½ (16.5)
    Avery Architectural Library, Columbia University, New York, New York, A. J. Davis Collection   C 1-1-v

Two of the four objects illustrated here, the wheel-back chair and the pedestal table, are still at Lyndhurst, the Alexander Jackson Davis-designed home for which they were originally intended (nos. 12 and 71). The origin of Davis's designs for these pieces is unclear but the source for the third, a straight-backed chair, is hardly original. Both Downing and Loudon illustrate very similar chairs in their design books. Davis's notations indicate he designed the four objects for the saloon (later the reception room) and one of the bedrooms.[1]
    KSH

1. Andrew Jackson Downing, *The Architecture of Country Houses*, 442; and John Claudius Loudon, *An Encyclopædia of Cottage, Farm, and Villa Architecture*, no. 661.

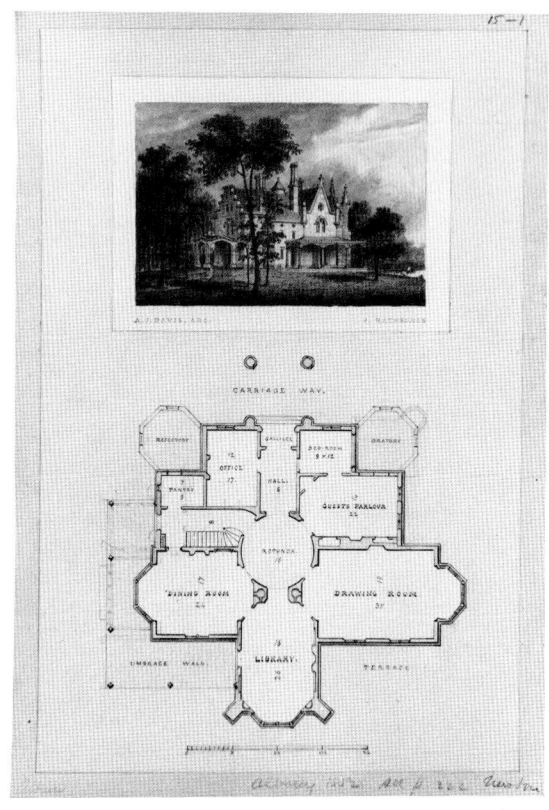

187

188

189

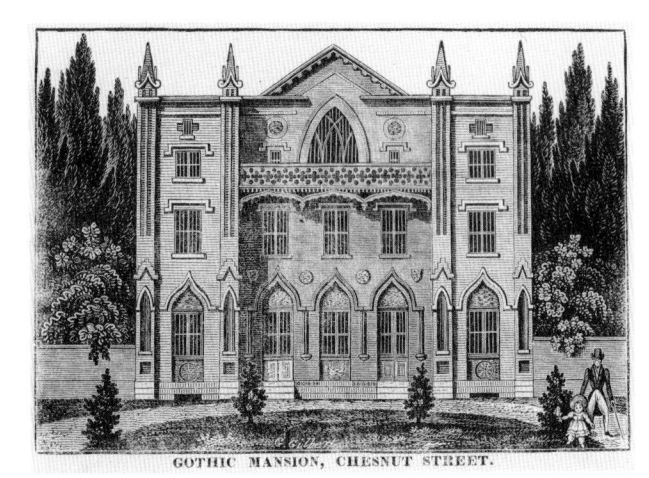

190

189 *Lyndehurst near Irvington*
Alexander Jackson Davis (1803–1892)
New York, New York, ca. 1864–1867
Watercolor on cardboard
H. 6⅜ (16.00) W. 4⅛ (10.50)
Avery Architectural Library, Columbia University, New York, New York, A. J. Davis Collection   X-4

In 1838 Alexander Jackson Davis began a project in Tarrytown, New York, that would involve him for almost three decades. In that year he started to design a "Country Mansion in Pointed Style, near Tarrytown, for Wm. Paulding and son Philip R. Paulding," one of the most outstanding Gothic Revival country houses built during America's romantic era.[1] Davis did his best to make "Knoll," "Paulding Manor," "Paulding Place," or "Lyndhurst," as it was variously known, a total Gothic Revival statement both inside and out. He included, on a grand scale, vaulted ceilings, pointed doorways, stained glass, and Gothic Revival furnishings. By the time Davis completed designing the house and its furnishings for Paulding, it was certainly one of the most elaborate, picturesque homes on the Hudson; yet when George Merritt bought Lyndhurst in 1864 he felt obliged to engage Davis again to double the mansion's size. This watercolor shows but one small detail of Merritt's house, the great tower. To the right of the tower Davis has added a very unmedieval, but very nineteenth-century, veranda.   KSH

1. *Lyndhurst, on the Hudson River, Tarrytown, N.Y.*, 14.

190 *Gothic Mansion, Chestnut Street*
Possibly engraved by George Gilbert (active ca. 1830)
Philadelphia, Pennsylvania, ca. 1830–1840
Ink on paper
H. 5 (12.70) W. 6 (15.24)
Mr. Lee B. Anderson

John Dorsey's home on Chestnut Street in Philadelphia was one of the first houses in the United States to receive a Gothic façade. Built about 1810, the house was actually fronted by a wealth of gingerbread superimposed on a traditional, classical interior. Unlike later dwellings, which at least attempted to be architecturally correct, Dorsey's house was entirely the concoction of a creative carpenter.

The woodcut of Dorsey's Gothic mansion is signed "G. Gilbert." The signature possibly refers to George Gilbert, a Philadelphia wood engraver who exhibited at the Pennsylvania Academy in 1831. Gilbert was listed in Philadelphia city directories from 1833 to 1849.[1]   KSH

1. George C. Groce and David H. Wallace, *The New-York Historical Society's Dictionary of Artists in America, 1564–1860*, p. 258.

191 *Suburban Gothic Villa, Murray Hill, N.Y. City. Residence of W. C. H. Waddell, Esq.*
Fanny Palmer, née Frances Flora Bond (ca. 1812–1876)
New York, New York, ca. 1844–1850
Lithograph on paper
H. 12 (30.48) W. 9 (22.86)
Mr. Lee B. Anderson

The fashionable Waddell House may have inspired Henry Harral when he commissioned Alexander Jackson Davis to design Walnut Wood in Bridgeport, Connecticut (no. 185). The exteriors are very nearly mirror images of each other. Davis designed William C. H. Waddell's house in that fashionable New York suburb, Murray Hill, on Fifth Avenue between 37th and 38th Streets. Evidently the great stone building was a conversation piece, because a lithograph of it was soon made by Fanny Palmer, a lithographer from Leicester, England, who immigrated to this country in the early 1840s and for many years was an artist for Currier and Ives.[1]   KSH

1. George C. Groce and David H. Wallace, *The New-York Historical Society's Dictionary of Artists in America, 1564–1860*, p. 485.

192 *Prospect Hill*

Karl Gildemeister (1820–1869), artist; Nagel and Weingaertner (active 1849–1856), engravers
New York, New York, 1849–1856
Lithograph on paper
H. 11½ (29.21) W. 14 (35.56)
Lyman Allyn Museum, New London, Connecticut   1971.7

Sometime between 1847, when a lithograph of the "old" Prospect Hill was published, and 1851, when steamboat-owner Lawrence M. Stevens died, Stevens capped his successful career by converting his controlled Greek Revival home into a castellated Gothic pile. Known as "Stevens Castle," Prospect Hill overlooked Norwalk, Connecticut, and its harbor. Its arched verandas, balustraded roof-line, and irregular tower successfully replaced the pediment, columned portico, and central tower that had trimmed the house before architect Joseph C. Wells, the designer of Roseland (no. 186), began his remodeling. Wells completed his Gothic scene with a crenelated out-kitchen on the left and a carriage house on the right.[1]

Karl Gildemeister, a German painter and lithographer, recorded Prospect Hill in its heyday, and Nagel and Weingaertner printed his rendering during their brief partnership between 1849 and 1856.[2] Stevens's widow continued to live at Prospect Hill until 1903. After an unfortunate sojourn as a rooming house, the mansion was destroyed by fire in 1917.

KSH

1. We are grateful to Ralph C. Bloom, curator of Lockwood House in Norwalk, Connecticut, for providing the above information.
2. George C. Groce and David H. Wallace, *The New-York Historical Society's Dictionary of Artists in America, 1564–1860*, pp. 259, 464.

193 *Sales Brochure*

Engraved by Anderson, ca. 1858
New York, New York, ca. 1858
Ink on paper
H. 13 (33.02) W. 11 (27.94)
Mr. Lee B. Anderson

"This block contains eleven independent dwellings, differing in size, price and amount of accommodation. They have from twelve to eighteen rooms each. The pile is altogether unique in its character and plan, the eleven dwellings being combined as in one palace . . . ." In 1858 Alexander Jackson Davis carried the Gothic Revival style five blocks up Fifth Avenue from the Waddell House (no. 191) to design one of the most remarkable Gothic Revival ventures of the day. His problem was simple and his solution was equally clear: if city dwellers neither wanted nor could afford Gothic castles in town, why not combine a row of houses under one Gothic façade to imitate a castellated palace? With neither moat nor lawn, Davis has created a picturesque, if deceiving, building. The eleven houses were built for speculation. To sell them Davis and the builder, George Higgins, must have ordered this sales brochure, which included on its masthead a woodcut of the building made by an unidentified engraver named Anderson.

KSH

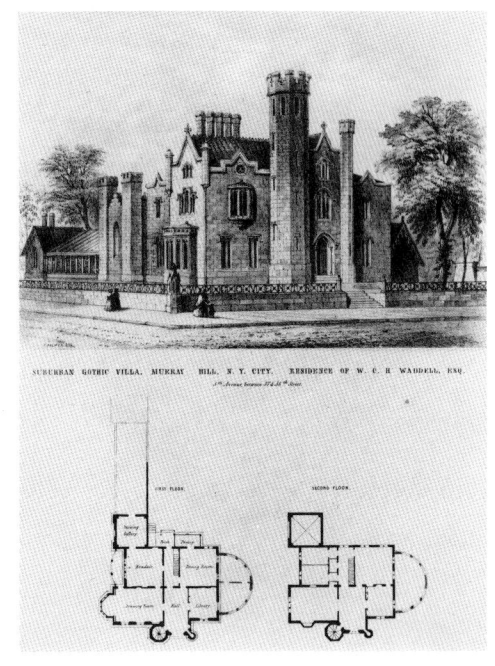

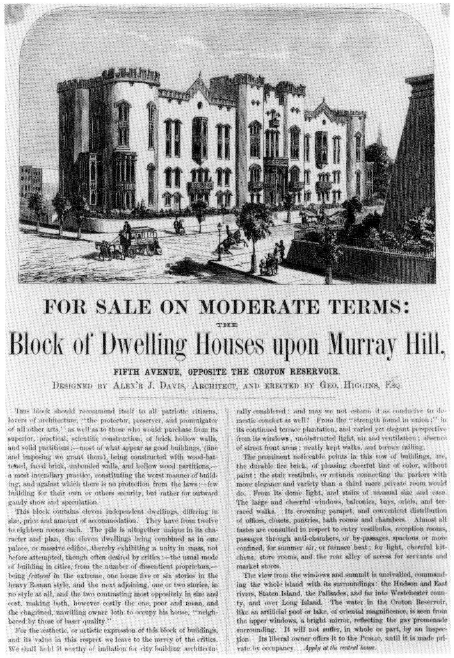

194

195

194 Daguerreotype Case
Probably United States, ca. 1845–1865
Leather on wood
H. 3⅝ (9.27) W. 3⅛ (7.95) D. ⅝ (1.65)
Hester Halstead Pier

Daguerreotypes were made by exposing a sensitized, polished, silvered copper plate to light. The image was developed by introducing heated mercury vapor to the surface. In order to protect the fragile surface from abrasion and further oxidation each daguerreotype had to be sealed and framed behind glass, thereby creating the need for a specialized product, the daguerreotype case. The cases themselves were imaginative indicators of popular taste. This one combines a turreted castle on a hill with a pleasant view of a sloop sailing below it. The image is a fairly common one that is also repeated on sandpaper (no. 182) and window shades (no. 150). KSH

195 Daguerreotype
United States, ca. 1845–1865
Silvered copper in a brass, glass, velvet, and leather case
Case Open: H. 3⅝ (9.27) W. 6⅜ (16.23) D. ⅝ (1.65)
Hester Halstead Pier

Light is that silent artist
Which without the aid of man
Designs on silver bright
Daguerre's immortal plan.[1]

When Louis Jacques Mandé Daguerre developed a method in France in 1838 to chemically fix images on silvered copper plates, he invented popular photography as we know it today. By 1840 the daguerreotype process had arrived in the United States, and such notables as Samuel F. B. Morse experimented with it.[2] Soon exposure times were reduced from ten to twenty minutes to ten to twenty seconds, making photography an appropriate vehicle for portraiture. The young girl photographed here sits in a very simple Gothic Revival child's chair with solid upholstered back and turned stiles, one modest enough to serve as a prop in a photographer's studio. Oblivious to her fancy seat, this child focuses on the photographer's wooden box and the prospect of having to stay absolutely still for an extended exposure time. KSH

1. Written by Dr. J. P. Simon (1839) as quoted in Helmut Gernsheim and Alison Gernsheim, *The History of Photography, from the Camera Obscura to the Beginning of the Modern Era* (New York, St. Louis, and San Francisco: McGraw-Hill Book Company, 1969), 72.
2. *Ibid.*, 120–129.

Glossary

ARCH†: a structural member (usually curved) that spans an opening and gives support by resolving vertical pressure into horizontal thrust
- CUSPED ARCH: a round arch topped by a smaller arc of approximately 180 degrees
- EQUILATERAL ARCH: an arch whose center point forms an angle approximating 90 degrees
- HORSESHOE ARCH: a round arch surmounted at the shoulder by an arc of approximately 270 degrees
- LANCET ARCH: a narrow arch whose center point forms an angle of less than 90 degrees
- OGEE ARCH: a pointed arch with tangent serpentines forming the vault
- ROUND ARCH: two vertical members joined by an arc approximating 180 degrees
- TREFOIL ARCH: a round arch topped by an equilateral or ogee arch
- TUDOR ARCH: a wide, low arch whose center point forms an angle approaching 180 degrees

BALUSTRADE†: a row of supports topped by a rail to serve as an open parapet along the edge of a balcony, roof, etc.

BARGEBOARD: see vergeboard

BRACKET: a projecting support designed to carry a vertical load or strengthen an angle, often carved and frequently merely decorative

BUTTRESS†: an external projecting structure for supporting or giving stability to a wall

CASTELLATED†: having designs or decorations resembling battlements

CLUSTERED COLUMNS: several thin columns joined together and serving as a unified post

CRENELATED†: having battlements

CORBEL†: a decorative drop projecting from a vertical surface, frequently at the base of an architectural termination

COTTAGE: a mid-nineteenth-century home suitable for the middle classes, frequently having between two and eight rooms

CROCKET†: an ornament, usually in the form of carved and bent foliage, used on the edge of a gable or spire, and adapted for similar use on furniture backs

DENTIL: one of a series of small projecting blocks, frequently decorating the underside of a roofline

LABEL: a heavy molding framing a window or door across its top edge and partly down its sides

MULLION: a divider between two sections in a window or opening

POINTED STYLE: a cottage in the Gothic Revival style exemplified by a steeply pitched roof, vertical board-and-batten (if in wood), and applied Gothic ornament

QUATREFOIL†: a heraldic representation of a flower with four petals, each of which is either rounded or pointed

ROSE WINDOW: a circular window with tracery, traditionally used on the west façade of cathedrals

SPANDREL†: the area between the arc of an arch and its next adjacent molding

TRACERY: originally decorative open work within Gothic framing, adapted as decorative detail in the nineteenth century

TREFOIL†: a heraldic representation having three leaves of lobes, each of which is either rounded or pointed

VERGEBOARD: a strip of wood, often elaborately carved, that ornaments the underside of a gable

VILLA: a substantial, upper-income, nineteenth-century home usually of brick or stone and found in the suburbs or country

†Entry adapted from *Webster's Third New International Dictionary of The English Language Unabridged* (Springfield, Mass.: G. and C. Merriam Co., 1966).

Selected Bibliography

Ackermann, Rudolph, ed. *The Repository of Arts, Literature, Fashions, Manufactures, etc.* Three Series. 40 vols. 1809–1828.

American Heritage History of American Antiques from the Revolution to the Civil War, The. Edited by Marshall B. Davidson. N.p.: American Heritage Publishing Co., 1968.

American Heritage History of Antiques from the Civil War to World War I, The. Edited by Marshall B. Davidson. N.p.: American Heritage Publishing Co., 1969.

Ames, Kenneth Leroy. "Renaissance Revival Furniture in America." Ph.D. dissertation, University of Pennsylvania, 1970.

Andrews, Wayne. "A Gothic Tragedy in Bridgeport?" *Antiques* LXXII (July 1957), 50–53.

———. *American Gothic: Its Origins, Its Trials, It Triumphs.* New York: Vintage Books, 1975.

Archer, Michael. "Gothic Wall-Papers: An Aspect of the Gothic Revival." *Apollo* LXXVIII (August 1963), 109–116.

Arnot, David Henry. *Gothic Architecture Applied to Modern Residences: Containing Designs of All the Important Parts of a Private Dwelling, Exhibited in Elaborate Perspective Drawings; Together with Large and Copious Details.* New York: D. Appleton and Company; Philadelphia: George S. Appleton, 1851.

Art and the Excited Spirit: America in the Romantic Period. Edited by David Carew Huntington, Edward R. Molnar, and Robert A. Yassin. Ann Arbor: University of Michigan Museum, 1972.

Aslin, Elizabeth. *Nineteenth Century English Furniture.* New York: Thomas Yoseloff, 1962.

Baker, Z. *Modern House Builder, from the Log Cabin and Cottage to the Mansion.* Boston: Higgins, Bradley, and Dayton, 1857.

Barret, Richard Carter. *Bennington Pottery and Porcelain: A Guide to Identification.* New York: Crown Publishers, 1958.

Biddle, James. "Nicholas Biddle's Andalusia, a Nineteenth Century Country Seat Today." *Antiques* LXXXVI (September 1964), 286–290.

Birmingham, Peter. *Jasper F. Cropsey, 1823–1900: A Retrospective View of America's Painter of Autumn.* College Park: University of Maryland Art Gallery, 1968.

Bowen, Henry C. "The Ledger of Henry C. Bowen." Manuscript in the collection of the Society for the Preservation of New England Antiquities, Boston, Mass.

Brooks, Samuel H. *Designs for Cottage and Villa Architecture: Containing Plans, Elevations, Sections, Perspective Views, and Details, for the Erection of Cottages and Villas.* London: Thomas Kelly, [1829].

Bryan, John Albury. "Molded Iron in the Middle West: A New Material in a New World One Hundred Years Ago." *Antiques* XLIII (January 1943), 79–81.

Butler, Joseph T. *American Antiques, 1800–1900: A Collector's History and Guide.* New York: Odyssey Press, 1965.

———. *Candleholders in America, 1650–1900: A Comprehensive Collection of American and European Candle Fixtures Used in America.* New York: Bonanza Books, 1967.

Cavalier, Julian. *American Castles.* South Brunswick, N. J., and New York: A. S. Barnes and Co.; London: Thomas Yoseloff, 1973.

Caveler, William. *Select Specimens of Gothic Architecture, Comprising the Most Approved Examples in England, from the Earliest to the Latest Date.* 2d ed. London: M. Taylor, 1839.

Clark, Kenneth. *The Gothic Revival: An Essay in the History of Taste.* Harmondsworth, England: Penguin Books, 1962.

Comstock, Helen. *American Furniture: Seventeenth, Eighteenth, and Nineteenth Century Styles.* New York: Viking Press, 1962.

———, ed. *The Concise Encyclopedia of American Antiques.* New York: Hawthorn Books, 1958.

Cooper, Jeremy. "Victorian Furniture: An Introduction to the Sources." *Apollo* XCV (February 1972), 115–122.

Davidson, Ruth. "Roseland, a Gothic Revival Mansion." *Antiques* LXXXI (May 1962), 510–514.

Davies, Jane B. "Llewellyn Park in West Orange, New Jersey." *Antiques* CVII (January 1975), 142–158.

Davis, Alexander Jackson. Papers. Manuscript material in the collections of Avery Architectural Library, Columbia University, New York; New York Public Library; Metropolitan Museum of Art, New York; and the Museum of the City of New York.

Downing, Andrew Jackson. *The Architecture of Country Houses: Including Designs for Cottages, and Farm-Houses, and Villas, with Remarks on Interiors, Furniture, and the Best Modes of Warming and Ventilating.* D. Appleton and Co., 1850. Reprint. New York: Dover Publications, 1969.

———. *Cottage Residences, Rural Architecture & Landscape Gardening.* New York and London:

Wiley and Putnam, Inc. Reprint. Watkins Glen, N. Y.: Library of Victorian Culture, 1967.

———. *Rural Essays*. Edited by George William Curtis. 1853. Reprint. New York: Da Capo Press, 1974.

———. *A Treatise on the Theory and Practice of Landscape Gardening, Adapted to North America; With a View to the Improvement of Country Residences.* New York and London: Wiley and Putnam, 1841; 2nd ed. New York and London: Wiley and Putnam, 1844; 5th ed. New York: G. P. Putnam, 1853.

Dunlap, William. *History of the Rise and Progress of the Arts of Design in the United States.* 2 vols. New York: George P. Scott and Co., 1834.

Eastlake, Charles Locke. *Hints on Household Taste in Furniture Upholstery and Other Details.* 4th ed. rev. London: Longmans, Green, and Co., 1878.

———. *A History of the Gothic Revival.* 1872. Reprint. Leicester, England: University Press, 1970.

Eastlake-Influenced American Furniture, 1870–1890. Yonkers, N. Y.: Hudson River Museum, 1973.

Eberlein, Harold Donaldson, and Hubbard, Cortlandt Van Dyke. "Living with Antiques: Nicholas Biddle's Andalusia." *Antiques* LXIII (April 1952), 339–342.

Fergusson, James. *The Illustrated Handbook of Architecture: Being a Concise and Popular Account of the Different Styles of Architecture Prevailing in all Ages and Countries.* 2 vols. London: John Murray, 1855.

Frangiamore, Catherine Lynn. "Wallpapers Used in Nineteenth-Century America." *Antiques* CII (December 1972), 1042–1051.

Frankl, Paul. *The Gothic: Literary Sources and Interpretations through Eight Centuries.* Princeton, N.J.: Princeton University Press, 1960.

Germann, Georg. *Gothic Revival in Europe and Britain: Sources, Influences and Ideas.* Cambridge, Mass.: M.I.T. Press, 1973.

Gloag, John. "Gentlemen's Gothic." *Antiques* XCV (May 1969), 682–688.

———. "Nineteenth-Century Gothic Furniture in England." *Antiques* CI (June 1972), 1046–1051.

———. *Victorian Comfort: A Social History of Design from 1830–1900.* New York: Macmillan Co., 1961.

Golovin, Anne Castrodale. *Bridgeport's Gothic Ornament: The Harral-Wheeler House.* Smithsonian Studies in History and Technology, 18. Washington, D.C.: Smithsonian Institution Press, 1972.

Goode, James M. "The Smithsonian Institution Building." Unpublished report, Smithsonian Institution, Washington, D.C., March 23, 1971.

Goodwin, Francis. *Domestic Architecture, Being a Second Series of Designs for Cottages, Lodges, Villas, and Other Residences, in the Grecian, Italian, and Old English Styles of Architecture.* London: By author, 1834.

———. *Rural Architecture: First Series of Designs for Rustic, Peasants', and Ornamental Cottages, Lodges, and Villas, in Various Styles of Architecture; Containing Fifty Plates.* 2d ed. London: John Weale, 1835.

Gothic Album for Cabinet Makers; Comprising a Collection of Designs for Gothic Furniture. Philadelphia: Henry Carey Baird, 1868.

'*Gothick.*' Brighton, England: Royal Pavilion, Art Gallery and Museums, 1975.

Gowans, Alan. *Images of American Living: Four Centuries of Architecture and Furniture as Cultural Expression.* Philadelphia and New York: J. B. Lippincott Co., 1964.

Groce, George C., and Wallace, David H. *The New-York Historical Society's Dictionary of Artists in America, 1564–1860.* New Haven and London: Yale University Press, 1957.

Hall, John. *The Cabinet Makers' Assistant, Embracing the Most Modern Style of Cabinet Furniture.* Baltimore: John Murphy, 1840. Reprint. N.p.: Harry Bland, 1944.

Hammond, J. H. *The Farmer's and Mechanic's Practical Architect; and Guide in Rural Economy.* Boston: John P. Jewett and Co.; Cleveland, Ohio: Henry P. B. Jewett, 1858.

Hawkins, John Sidney. *An History of the Origin and Establishment of Gothic Architecture.* London: J. Taylor, 1813.

Hersey, George L. *High Victorian Gothic: A Study in Associationism.* Baltimore and London: Johns Hopkins University Press, 1972.

Higgins, William Mullingar. *The House Painter; or Decorator's Companion: A Complete Treatise on the Origin of Colour, the Laws of Harmonious Colouring, the Manufacture of Pigments, Oils, and Varnishes; and the Art of House Painting, Graining, and Marbling. To Which is Added, a History of the Art in All Ages.* London: Thomas Kelly, 1841.

Hitchcock, Henry-Russell. *American Architectural Books: A List of Books, Portfolios, and Pamphlets on Architecture and Related Subjects Published in America before 1895.* 3rd rev. ed. Minneapolis: University of Minnesota, 1946.

Ireland, LeRoy. *The Works of George Inness: An Illustrated Catalogue Raisonné.* Austin and London: University of Texas Press, 1965.

Jones, Owen. *The Grammar of Ornament.* London: Bernard Quaritch, 1868.

Kenney, Alice P., and Workman, Leslie J. "Ruins, Romance, and Reality: Medievalism in Anglo-American Imagination and Taste, 1750–1840." In *Winterthur Portfolio 10*, edited by Ian M. G. Quimby, pp. 131–163. Charlottesville: University Press of Virginia, 1975.

Kopp, Joel, and Kopp, Kate. *Hooked Rugs in the Folk Art Tradition.* New York: Museum of American Folk Art, 1974.

Lamps & Other Lighting Devices, 1850–1906. Compiled by the editors of the Pyne Press. Princeton, N.J.: Pyne Press, 1972.

Lang, William Bailey. *Views, with Ground Plans, of the Highland Cottages at Roxbury, (Near Boston,) Designed and Erected by W. Bailey Lang.* Boston: L. H. Bridgham and H. E. Felch, 1845.

Langley, Batty, and Langley, Thomas. *Gothic Architecture Improved by Rules and Proportions.* London: Millais, 1747. Reprint. Farnborough, England: Gregg Press, 1967.

Lichten, Frances. *Decorative Art of Victoria's Era.* New York and London: Charles Scribner's Sons, 1950.

Little, Nina Fletcher. *American Decorative Wall Painting, 1700–1850.* New York: E. P. Dutton and Co., 1972.

Loth, Calder, and Sadler, Julius Trousdale, Jr. *The Only Proper Style: Gothic Architecture in America.* Boston: New York Graphic Society, 1975.

Loudon, John Claudius. *An Encyclopædia of Cottage, Farm, and Villa Architecture and Furniture; Containing Numerous Designs for Dwellings, from the Villa to the Cottage and the Farm, Including Farm Houses, Farmeries, and Other Agricultural Buildings; Country Inns, Public Houses, and Parochial Schools.* New ed. London: Longmans, Green, and Co., 1867.

Lyndhurst, On the Hudson River, Tarrytown, N.Y. Washington, D.C.: National Trust for Historic Preservation, 1973. Reprint of *Historic Preservation* XVII (March–April 1965).

Maass, John. *The Gingerbread Age: A View of Victorian America.* New York and Toronto: Rinehart and Company, 1957.

―――. *The Victorian Home in America.* New York: Hawthorn Books, 1972.

Mackenzie, Frederick, and Pugin, Augustus Charles. *Specimens of Gothic Architecture Consisting of Doors, Windows, Buttresses, Pinnacles &c; With Measurements Selected from Ancient Buildings at Oxford &c.* London: J. Taylor, [1845].

Mallach, Stanley. "Gothic Furniture Designs by Alexander Jackson Davis." Master's thesis, University of Delaware, 1966.

McCabe, James D. *The Illustrated History of the Centennial Exhibition.* Philadelphia, Chicago, and St. Louis: National Publishing Co., 1876.

McClinton, Katharine Morrison. "Furniture and Interiors Designed by A. J. Davis." *Connoisseur* CLXX (January 1969), 54–61.

McKearin, George S., and McKearin, Helen. *American Glass.* New York: Crown Publishers, 1948.

Merritt, Howard S. *Thomas Cole.* Rochester, N.Y.: Memorial Art Gallery of the University of Rochester, 1969.

Montgomery, Charles F. *American Furniture: The Federal Period.* New York: Viking Press, 1966.

―――. "John Needles—Baltimore Cabinetmaker." *Antiques* LXV (April 1954), 292–295.

Morris, Nathalie Lorillard Bailey. "Collection of Photographs of Gothic Revival Houses in New York City and the Eastern Parts of the U. S., Mainly by Alexander Jackson Davis." Unpublished material deposited at Avery Architectural Library, Columbia University, New York.

Newton, Roger Hale. *Town & Davis, Architects: Pioneers in American Revivalist Architecture, 1812–1870.* New York: Columbia University Press, 1942.

19th-Century America: Furniture and Other Decorative Arts. New York: Metropolitan Museum of Art, 1970.

19th-Century America: Paintings and Sculpture. New York: Metropolitan Museum of Art, 1970.

Ormsbee, Thomas H. *Field Guide to American Victorian Furniture.* Boston and Toronto: Little, Brown and Company, 1952.

Otto, Celia Jackson. *American Furniture of the Nineteenth Century.* New York: Viking Press, 1965.

―――. "Pillar and Scroll: Greek Revival Furniture of the 1830's." *Antiques* LXXXI (May 1962), 504–507.

Patton, Glenn. "James Keys Wilson (1828–1894): Architect of the Gothic Revival in Cincinnati." *Journal of the Society of Architectural Historians* XXVI (December 1967), 285–293.

Pearce, John N. "A. J. Davis' Greatest Gothic." *Antiques* LXXXVII (June 1965), 684–689.

―――. "Transatlantic Neo-Gothic: A. J. Davis' Designs for Lyndhurst, 1838–47, 1864–67." *Connoisseur* CLXX (March 1969), 179–187.

Pearce, John N., and Pearce, Lorraine W. "More on the Meeks Cabinetmakers." *Antiques* XC (July 1966), 69–73.

Pearce, John N.; Pearce, Lorraine W.; and Smith, Robert C. "The Meeks Family of Cabinetmakers." *Antiques* LXXXV (April 1964), 414–420.

Peterson, Harold L. *Americans at Home, from the Colonists to the Late Victorians: A Pictorial Source Book of American Domestic Interiors with an Appendix on Inns and Taverns.* New York: Charles Scribner's Sons, 1971.

Poe, Edgar Allan. "Philosophy of Furniture." In *Masterful Essays: Fanciful, Humorous and Serious,* pp. 11–20. New York and Akron, Ohio: D. M. Mac Lellan Book Company, n.d.

Price, Uvedale. *An Essay on the Picturesque, as Compared with the Sublime and the Beautiful; And, the Use of Studying Pictures, for the Purpose of Improving Real Landscape.* London: J. Robson, 1794.

Pugin, Augustus Charles. *Specimens of Gothic Architecture; Selected from Various Ancient Edifices in England: Consisting of Plans, Elevations, Sections, and Parts at Large.* 2 vols. London: M. A. Nattali, [1825?].

Pugin, Augustus Welby Northmore. *Designs for Gold & Silversmiths.* London: Ackermann and Co., 1836.

―――. *Design for Iron & Brass Work in the Style of the XV and XVI Centuries.* London: Ackermann and Co., 1836.

―――. *Details of Antient Timber Houses of the 15th and 16th Centuries Selected from Those Existing at Rouen, Caen, Beauvais, Gisors, Abbeville, Strasbourg, etc.* London: Ackermann and Co., 1836.

―――. *Gothic Furniture in the Style of the 15th Century.* London: Ackermann and Co., 1835.

―――. *The True Principles of Pointed or Christian Architecture: Set Forth in Two Lectures Delivered at St. Marie's Oscott.* London: John Weale, 1841.

Rabinowitz, Polly. "Life at Roseland: Bowens and Holts." Manuscript in the possession of the Society for the Preservation of New England Antiquities, Boston, Mass., 1971.

Ranlett, William H. *The Architect, A Series of Original Designs, for Domestic and Ornamental Cottages and Villas, Connected with Landscape Gardening, Adapted to the United States.* Vol. I. New York: Dewitt and Davenport, 1849.

Repton, Humphry. *The Landscape Gardening and Landscape Architecture of the Late Humphry Repton, Esq.: Being His Entire Works on These Subjects.* New ed. introduced by J. C. Loudon. London: Longman and Co.; Edinburgh: A. and C. Black, 1840.

Ritch, John W. *The American Architect: Comprising Original Designs of Cheap Country and Village Residences, with Details, Specifications, Plans and Directions, and an Estimate of the Cost of Each Design.* New York: C. M. Saxton, 1852.

Robinson, Peter Frederick. *Designs for Ornamental Villas.* 3d ed. London: Henry G. Bohn, 1836.

_____. *A New Series of Designs for Ornamental Cottages and Villas, with Estimates of the Probable Cost of Erecting Them; Forming a Sequel to the Works Entitled* Rural Architecture *and* Designs for Ornamental Villas. London: Henry G. Bohn, 1838.

_____. *Rural Architecture: Being a Series of Designs for Ornamental Cottages.* 3d ed. London: James Carpenter and Son, 1828.

Schimmelman, Janice Gayle. "The American Taste for Gothic Architecture: Poetic Literature and Architectural Criticism in the Nineteenth Century." Master's thesis, University of Michigan, 1972.

Scott, Walter. *Ivanhoe: A Romance.* 2d ed. 3 vols. Edinburgh: A. Constable and Co., 1820.

_____. *Lady of the Lake, The.* Edinburgh: John Ballantyne and Co., 1810.

Shaw, Edward. *The Modern Architect.* Boston: Dayton, 1854.

Sloan, Samuel. *American Houses: A Variety of Original Designs for Rural Buildings.* Philadelphia: Henry B. Ashmead, 1861.

Smith, George. *The Cabinet-Maker and Upholsterer's Guide: Being a Complete Drawing Book; in Which Will Be Comprised Treatises on Geometry and Perspective, as Applicable to the Above Branches of Mechanics, . . . to Which Is Added, a Complete Series of New and Original Designs for Household Furniture, and Interior Decoration.* London: Jones and Co., 1826.

Smith, Robert C. "The Furniture of Anthony G. Quervelle, Part I: The Pier Tables," *Antiques* CIII (May 1973), 984–994; "Part II: The Pedestal Tables," *Antiques* CIV (July 1973), 90–99; "Part III: The Worktables," *Antiques* CIV (August 1973), 260–268; "Part IV: Some Case Pieces," *Antiques* CV (January 1974), 180–193; "Part V: Sofas, Chairs, and Beds," *Antiques* CV (March 1974), 512–521.

_____. "Gothic and Elizabethan Revival Furniture, 1800–1850." *Antiques* LXXV (March 1959), 272–276.

_____. "Philadelphia Empire Furniture by Antoine Gabriel Quervelle." *Antiques* LXXXVI (September 1964), 304–309.

Spofford, Harriet Prescott. "Mediaeval Furniture." *Harper's New Monthly Magazine* LIII (November 1876), 809–829.

Stanton, Phoebe B. *The Gothic Revival & American Church Architecture: An Episode in Taste, 1840–1856.* Baltimore: Johns Hopkins Press, 1968.

Susman, Katherine B. "Gothic Revival Domestic Architecture in Cooperstown, New York, 1834–1868: The Evolution of a Style." Master's thesis, State University of New York, College at Oneonta, 1971.

Talbert, Bruce J. *Gothic Forms Applied to Furniture, Metal Work and Decoration for Domestic Purposes.* Boston: J. R. Osgood and Co., 1873.

Tatum, George Bishop. "Andrew Jackson Downing: Arbiter of American Taste, 1815–1852." Ph.D. dissertation, Princeton University, 1949.

Trendall, E. W. *Original Designs for Cottages and Villas in the Grecian, Gothic and Italian Styles of Architecture.* London: By author, 1831.

Upjohn, Richard. *Upjohn's Rural Architecture: Designs, Working Drawings and Specifications for a Wooden Church, and Other Rural Structures.* New York: George P. Putnam, 1852. Reprint. New York: Da Capo Press, 1975.

Vaux, Calvert. "Hints for Country House Builders." *Harper's New Monthly Magazine* XI (November 1855), 763–778.

_____. *Villas and Cottages: A Series of Designs Prepared for Execution in the United States.* 2d ed. New York, 1864. Reprint. New York: Dover Publications, 1970.

Victorian Cabinet-Maker's Assistant: 418 Original Designs with Descriptions and Details of Construction, The. 1853. Reprint. New York: Dover Publications, 1970.

Wainwright, Clive. "A. W. N. Pugin's Early Furniture." *Connoisseur* CXCI (January 1976), 3–11.

Waite, John G., and Waite, Diana S. "Stovemakers of Troy, New York." *Antiques* CIII (January 1973), 144.

Walter, Thomas Ustick, and Smith, John Jay. *Two Hundred Designs for Cottages and Villas.* Philadelphia: Carey and Hart, 1846.

Webster, Thomas, and Parkes, Mrs. [William]. *An Encyclopædia of Domestic Economy: Comprising Subjects Connected with the Interests of Every Individual; Such as the Construction of Domestic Edifices; Furniture; Carriages, and Instruments of Domestic Use.* Edited by D. M. Reese. New York: Harper and Brothers, 1855.

Westcott, Thompson. *Centennial Portfolio: A Souvenir of the International Exhibition at Philadelphia, Comprising Lithographic Views of Fifty of Its Principal Buildings, with Letter-Press Description.* Philadelphia: Thomas Hunter, 1876.

Wheeler, Gervase. *Homes for the People, in Suburb and Country; the Villa, the Mansion, and the Cottage, Adapted to American Climate and Wants.* New York: Charles Scribner, 1855.

Wood, Henry. *A Series of Designs of Furniture & Decoration in the Styles of Louis XVIth, Francis 1st, Elizabeth, and Gothic.* London: W. Pickering, [1845].

Woodward, George E. *Woodward's Architecture and Rural Art.* New York: George E. Woodward, 1867.

_____. *Woodward's Country Homes.* New York: George E. Woodward, 1865.

_____. *Woodward's Natural Architect; Containing 1000 Original Designs, Plans and Details, to Working Scale, for the Practical Construction of Dwelling Houses for the Country, Suburb and Village.* New York: George E. Woodward, 1869.

Index

(Illustration numbers are printed in boldface type.)

Abbotsford, Melrose, England, 4, **180**
Ackermann, Rudolph, 70, **104**
Afton Villa, Saint Francisville, Louisiana, 6
Albany, New York, 73, **150**, **158**
American Clock Company (ca. 1835-1855), **113**
American Pottery Manufacturing Company, **142**
Andalusia, Bucks County, Pennsylvania
    bed at, **93**, **104**
    chairs at, **8**, **9**
    grotto of, **183**
    hall bench at, **52**
Anderson, Mr., **193**
Andrews, Franklin C., **113**
Arbury Hall, Warwickshire, England, 2
Architecture of Country Houses, The (Downing), 73, 96
Argand, Ami, **116**
Auburn, New York, **110**

Bakewell and Company (1808-1882), **123**
Baltimore, Maryland
    bookcase from, **90**
    desk from, **78**
    tables from, **62**, **63**
    Warner silver from, **144**
Barrow, David, 6
Barry, Joseph B., 8
Bates, Edward, **176**
Beecher, Henry Ward, 6
Belmead, Powahatan County, Virginia, 7
Belter, John Henry, **58**
Bennington, Vermont, **141**
Biddle, Nicholas, 8, 9, **93**, **183**
Bigelow Chapel, Cambridge, Massachusetts, **115**
Blithewood, Barrytown, New York, 4
Bonaparte, Jerome Napolean, **63**
Bonaparte, Joseph, **93**, **104**
Bolton, Rev. Robert, 4
Boston, Massachusetts, 3, 4, 79
    bottles from, **135-137**
    candlesticks from, **115**

chair from, **18**
compote from, **124**
decanter from, **122**
dishes from, **125**, **126**, **128**
painters and, **169**, **172**
pitcher from, **121**
sugar bowls from, **130**
Boston and Sandwich Glass Company, **122**, **124-126**, **128**, **130**
Bowen, Henry Chandler (1813-1896), 6, **6**, **21**, **53**, **57**, **58**, **72**, **85**, **95**, **106**, **186**
Bradley, Joseph, **21**
Brewton, Miles, House, Charleston, South Carolina, 3
Brooklyn, New York
    chairs from, **1**, **20-22**, **42**
    footstool from, **58**
    garden bench from, **59**
    hall stand from, **106**
    settees from, **56**, **57**
    window seat from, **53**
Brooks, Thomas (1811-1887), **72**
    chairs by, **20-22**, **42**
    footstool by, **58**
    hall stand by, **106**
    settees by, **56**, **57**
    window seat by, **53**
Brown, Jonathan Clark (1807-1872), **112**
Bryant, William Cullen, 1, **168**
Bufford, John H., **184**
Burns, William, **12**
Burns and Tranque (Trainque), **12 and n**
Byrne, Richard, **12**

Camac, Turner, 4
Cargill, Henry A., **116**
Carpenter, Francis Bicknell (1830-1900), **176**, **177**
Carter, Mr. and Mrs. Charles Henry Augustus, **173**
Castlewood, Llewellyn Park, New Jersey, 7
Chippendale, Thomas, 2
Church, Frederick Edwin, **170**

Civil War, 1, **176**
Clark, William Starr, **116**
Clark, Coit, and Cargill (1833-1836), **116**
Classical style, 1, 2, **81**
Clover, Lewis, P., **184**
Cocke, Philip St. George, 7
Coit, Thomas C., **116**
Cole, Thomas C. (1801-1848), **166-168**, **170**, **180**, **181**
Cooper, James Fenimore, 1, 4, **184**. See also Otsego Hall, Cooperstown, New York
Cooper family (Cooperstown, New York), 65
Cornelius, Christian (active after 1810), **118**
Cornelius and Company (active 1840-1855), **118**
Country Scene, **180**
Cox, James, **145**
Cox, John, **145**
Cropsey, Jasper Francis (1823-1900), **180**
Crystal Palace Exhibition, **141**
Currier and Ives, **191**

Daguerre, Louis Jacques Mandé, **195**
Daingerfield family (Baltimore), **62**
Daniels, Albe C., **30**, **49**
Daniels and Hitchins (active 1850-1868), **30**, **49**
Davis, Alexander Jackson (1803-1892)
    collaboration of, with Downing, 5
    on English designs, 2
    furniture designs of, 9, **10**, **14**, **46**, **73**, **105**
    and Harral-Wheeler House, **19**, **97**, **111**, **185**
    houses designed by 4, 5-6, 7, 10, **41**, **60**, **105**, **186**, **191**, **193**
    Lyndhurst bed design of, **96**
    Lyndhurst chair designs of, **11-13**, **15-17**
    Lyndhurst table designs of, **69 and n**, **70**, **71**
    sketches of, for Lyndhurst, **188**, **189**
Davis, Joseph Beale, **10**, **12n**, **96**
Davis, W. H., **136**, **137**
Delamater, Henry, 5
Delano family (Barrytown, New York), **49**
Departure, The, **167**

98

Design for Grotto at Mr. Biddles Country Seat, **183**
Director, The Gentleman and Cabinet-Maker's (Chippendale), 3
Doane, George Washington, 8
Dorsey, John, 4, **190**
Doughty, Thomas (1793–1856), **169**
Downing, Andrew Jackson (1815–1852)
    books of, 6, 7, **73**, **96**, **173**, **188**
    on Gothic architecture, 1, **111**, **114**, **158**, **163**, **186**, **187**
    Gothic terms of, 10, **23**
    life of, 5
    taste of, in interior decoration, 5, **52**, **60**, **86**, **89**, **153**
"Downing cottages," 5
Downton, Herefordshire, England, 3
Dunlap, William, **172**

Eagleton, Florence Peshine, **38**
Eastlake, Charles, **17**, **59**, **70**, **109**, **119**
Ecclesiologists, 3, 10
Eddy, George W. (active 1853–1875), **157**
Empire period, influence of, **1**, **8**, **100**
Encyclopædia of Domestic Economy, **108**
England, influence of, on American revival, 1, 2, 3, 4
Ericstan, Tarrytown, New York, 7
Esher Lodge, Surrey, England, 10

Fanciful Landscape, **169**
Fight below the Battlements, **171**
Finney-Johnson Plantation, Buchanan, Virginia, **159**
First Reading of the Emancipation Proclamation, **176**, **177**
Fisher and Company, New York, **105**
Font Hill, Yonkers, New York, 6
Fonthill Abbey, Wiltshire, England, 2
Forestville Manufacturing Company (1835–1855), **112**
Fowler, Samuel P., House, Danversport, Massachusetts, **152**
Freeman, Hannah Lum, **31**
Frost, Peterson Company, **51**

Gale, William (1799–1867), **143**
Gale and Hughes, and William Gale and Son (active 1845–1860), **143**
Gardner and Company, New York, **51**
Gerard, James, W., 7
Gilbert, George (active 1830–1850), **190**
Gildemeister, Karl (1820–1869), **192**
Gilmor, Robert, 4
Gilpin, Henry D., **78**
Glen Ellen, Baltimore, Maryland, 4
Glenn Cottage, Roxbury, Massachusetts, **23**
"Gothick," 2, 8, 9n, **118**, **183**
Gothic Mansion, Chestnut Street, **190**

Gould, Jay, **96**
Grace Church, New York, New York, 7
Gracie family (New York), **50**, **54**
Greatbach, Daniel, **142**
Green-Meldrim House, Savannah, Georgia, 7
Greenwood Lake, New Jersey, **180**

Hagley Hall, Staffordshire, England, **183**
Hallock, Gerard (1800–1866), 4, **178**
Hallock House. 1836., **178**
Harding, Chester (1792–1866), **172**
Harral, Henry Kollock (1808–1854), 7, **96**, **185**, **191**
Harral-Wheeler House, Bridgeport, Connecticut
    architecture of, **19**, **111**, **185**, **191**
    furniture from, **19**, **55**, **86**, **96**, **97**, **103**, **105**
Harral-Wheeler House, The, **185**
Harvey, George, 4
Hazard family, **4**
Henderson, David, **142**
Henkels, George J. (active 1843–1877), **34**
Herrick, John J., 7
Higgins, George, **193**
Hill, John William, **184**
Hitchins, John, **30**, **49**
"House of Mansions," 7
Houses of Parliament (1836–1860), 3
Howard, Joseph, 7
Hudson River School, 1, **170**. SEE ALSO under individual artists
Hudson River Valley, New York, 4, 5, **3**, **163**
Huiskamp, Mr. and Mrs. John M., **27**
Hurst-Pierrepont House, Garrison, New York, 7, **41**
Hutton, Pelatiah M. (active 1848–1852), **99**

Ingleside, Dobbs Ferry, New York, 7, **105**
Inness, George (1825–1894), **170**
Iranistan, Bridgeport, Connecticut, **185**
Irving, Washington, 4, **3**, **170**, **186**
Ivanhoe, **114**

James, John B., 10
Jelliff, John (1813–1893), **38**, **39**, **174**
Jelliff, Mary Marsh, **38**
Jersey Porcelain and Earthenware Company, **142**
Johnson, Andrew, 4
Johnson, John E., 6

Kelly, Robert (1808–1856), **42**, **67**
Kennedy, David S., 8
Kent, William, 2, 10
Kenwood, **187**
Kenwood, Albany, New York, 7, **73**, **187**

Kenyon College, Gambier, Ohio, 4
Keyes, Frances Parkinson, **87**, **88**
Keyes, Mrs. Henry, **87**
Kingscote, Newport, Rhode Island, 6
Kittell, Nicholas Biddle (1822–1894), **173**
Knight, Richard Payne, 3
Knoll, 7. SEE ALSO Lyndhurst, Tarrytown, New York

Lacock Abbey, Wiltshire, England, 10
Lancelot, **114**
Langley, Batty, 2
Latrobe, Benjamin H., 4
Lawrence, Mrs. Abbott, **172**
Leatherstocking Tales, **184**
Lee Priory, 2
Lenox, James, 7
Lewis, W. K., and Brothers, **135**
Lincoln, Abraham, 4, **176**
Lithgow, James Smith (1812–1902), **175**
Livingston, Herman Thong (Tong), **88**
Livingston, Fox and Company, **88**
Long Island City, New York, **88**
Longfellow, Henry Wadsworth, **33**
Longstreet, C. Tyler, 6
Loudon, John Claudius, **19**, **98**, **188**
Louisville, Kentucky, **175**
Ludlow, Thomas, 4
Lum, Amos (1792–1862), **31**
Lum, Samuel Y., **31**
Lyman, Fenton and Company, **141**
Lyndehurst near Irvington, **189**
Lyndhurst, Tarrytown, New York, **173**
    bed at, **96**, **97**
    chairs at, **12-15**, **17**
    Davis designs of, 5, **188**
    tables at, **69-71**
    tower of, 7, **189**
Lyon, Samuel E., **15**, **59**, **70**

Massachusetts, **37**. SEE ALSO Boston, Massachusetts
McKee, Frederick, **133**
McKee, James, **133**
McKee Factory, **133**
Mediterranean Coast Scene with Tower, **166**
Meeks, John and Joseph W. (1836–1860)
    chairs of, **3**, **4**, **26**, **45**, **176**, **177**
    couch of, **54**
    desk and bookcase of, **82**
    payment voucher of, **5**
    sideboard of, **80**
    table of, **76**

Meeks, Joseph, and Sons (1829–1835), **64**, **81**
Meeks family (New York), **50**
Merritt, George, 7, **15**, **17**, **96**, **189**. SEE ALSO Lyndhurst, Tarrytown, New York
Middle Ages, influence of, on Gothic Revival, 1, 2, 3, 8, 7, **12**, **53**, **127**
Middle West, **127**, **129**
Millbrook, Tarrytown, New York, 5
Miller, Henry H., **38**
Miller, Sanderson, 2, 10, **183**
Miller Iron Company, **164**, **165**
Milligan, Robert J., **30 and n**
Milligan, Sarah, F., **30**
Morse, Samuel F. B., **195**

Nagel and Weingaertner (active 1849–1856), **192**
Nash, John, 3
Natchez, Mississippi, **48**
National Academy of Design, **171**, **180**, **185**
Needles, John (1786–1878), **62**, **63**
New England. SEE ALSO under individual cities and states
    furniture from, **6**, **19**, **55**, **85**, **95**, **103**
    interior accessories from, **154**, **163**, **179**
    painters in, **172**, **178**
    salt dish from, **132**
New England Glass Company, **121**
New Orleans, Louisiana, **88**, **91**
New York. SEE ALSO New York, New York
    bed from, **95**
    chairs from, **6**, **19**, **27**, **28**, **41**
    couch from, **55**
    dresser from, **85**
    footscraper from, **163**
    overmantel mirror from, **103**
    painters in, **166-168**, **170**, **173**, **176**, **181**
    tables from, **67**, **68**, **73**, **74**, **77**
    window shades from, **150**
New York, New York, 3, 4, **88**, **193**
    argand lamps from, **116**
    armchairs from, **15**, **17**, **26**
    artists in, **16**, **184**, **187**, **191**, **192**
    beds from, **96**, **97**
    bench from, **59**
    couch from, **54**
    Davis architecture in, **111**, **185**, **186**, **188**, **189**
    desk and bookcase from, **82**
    hall chairs from, **13**, **45**
    manufacturers in, **12**, **113**, **155**, **177**
    piano stool from, **50**
    pier glass from, **105**
    rocking chair from, **51**
    side chairs from, **2**, **4**, **10-12**, **14**, **36**
    silver from, **143**, **145**
    tables from, **64**, **69-72**, **75**
    whatnot from, **89**
New York World's Fair (1853), **185**
Newark, New Jersey, **31**, **38**, **39**, **174**
Newburgh, New York, 5, **170**
Newdigate, Sir Roger, 2
Notman, John, 8
Nott, Eliphalet (1773–1866), **151**, **155**
Noyes and Hutton (active 1848-1852), **99**

Oak Bluffs, Martha's Vineyard, Massachusetts, 6
Oaklands, Kennebec, Maine, 4
Ormsbee, Thomas, **47**
Otsego County, New York, **65**
Otsego Hall, **184**
Otsego Hall, Cooperstown, New York, 4, **65**, **184**

Palmer, Fanny (née Frances Flora Bond), **191**
Parker, Theodore, **79**
Patterson Elizabeth, **63**
Paulding, Philip R., 5, **12**, **13**, **96**, **189**. SEE ALSO Lyndhurst, Tarrytown, New York
Paulding, William, 5, **96**, **189**. SEE ALSO Lyndhurst, Tarrytown, New York
Pennington, William, 7
Percival, John, **110**
Perkins, Edward Newton, 6
Perpendicular period, 3
Peshine, Mary C. P. Jelliff, **38**
Philadelphia, Pennsylvania, 3, 4, 9, **51**, **190**
    astral lamp from, **118**
    bench from, **52**
    chairs from, **7-9**, **34**, **44**
    firedogs from, **161**
    music cabinet from, **84**
    pier glass from, **100**
    Tucker vase from, **140**
    Walter in, **183**
Picturesque theory, 1–3, 5, 6, 8
Pierrepont, Edwards, 7
Pinebank, Jamaica Plain, Massachusetts, 6
Pittsburgh, Pennsylvania, **123**, **133**
Pittsburgh Flint Glass Manufactory of Bakewell and Company (1808-1882), **123**
Poe, Edgar Allan, **181**
Point Breeze, Bordentown, New Jersey, **93**, **104**
Polk, James K., 4
Pratt, Enoch, House, Baltimore, Maryland, **90**
Priory, New Rochelle, New York, 4

Prospect Hill, **192**
Providence, Rhode Island, **26**, **164**, **165**
Pugin, Augustus Welby Northmore, 3, 10, **14**, **70**, **71**, **87**, **152**

Quervelle, Anthony G. (1789-1856), 7, **84**

Rathbone, Joel, 7, **73 and n**, **187**
Renwick, James, Jr. (1818–1895), 6, 7, **23**, **24**
Renwick, Robert (active 1837–1890), **90**
Restauration style, influence of
    on beds, **91**, **92**, **95**
    on case pieces, **80**, **81**, **84**
    on chairs, **1-4**, **7**, **21**, **44**, **176**
    on furnishings, **173**
    on pier glass, **100**
    on stool, **50**
    on table, **62**
Return, The, **168**
Revival styles
    Bracketed, 1
    Egyptian, 1
    Elizabethan, 1, **76**
    Gothic, defined, 9n
    in England, 1–3
    Greek, 1, **48**, **183**, **192**
    Italianate, 1, 8
    Norman, **23**
    Renaissance, 1, **58**, **66**, **69**, **74**
    Rococo, 1, **40**, **41**, **43**, **58**, **66**, **91**, **114**, **126**
    Romantic, 1, 2
    Rural Gothic, 4, 5
    Swiss, 1
    Tudor Gothic, 5
Ritchie, Alexander Hay, **177**
Riverside, Burlington, New Jersey, 8
Rockingham ware, **141**
Rokeby, Barrytown, New York, 8
Rosa, Salvator, 3
Roseland, **186**
Roseland, Woodstock, Connecticut, **6**, **173**, **192**
    architecture of, 6, **21**, **186**
    bed at, **95**
    dresser and mirror at, **85**
    hall stand for, **106**
    seating furniture for, **21**, **22**, **53**, **56**, **57**
    table at, **72**
Rotch, William J., 5, **163**
Roux, Alexander (active 1837–1881), **2**, **3**, **36**
Roux, Frederick (active 1847–1849), **2**, **3**
Ruined Castle by a Bay, **181**

Rural Residences (Davis), 4
Ruskin, John, 3

Sanford, Gideon, **89n**
Savery and Company (ca. 1839–1869), **161**
Scott, Sir Walter, 2, **114, 146, 180**
Sedgeley, Philadelphia, Pennsylvania, 4
Shaw, William F. (ca. 1845–1900), **115**
Sheldon, Henry, 5
Shepard, Helen Gould, **96**
Shepard and Company (ca. 1842–1848), **155**
Smith, Caleb B., **176**
Smith, Caroline E., **37**
Smithsonian Institution, design of, **23**
Spencer, Lilly Martin (1822–1902), **174**
Stanton, Frederick, **48**
Stanton Hall, Natchez, Mississippi, **48, 107**
Staunton Hill, Charlotte County, Virginia, 6
Steen Valetje, Barrytown, New York, **49**
Stevens, Lawrence M., **192**
Stone, Sidney M., 4, **178**
Strange, Edwin B., 7, **105**
Strawberry Hill, Twickenham, England, 2, 4
Stuart, Gilbert, **172**
Sturgis and Brigham, 6
Suburban Gothic Villa, Murray Hill, N.Y. City, Residence of W. C. H. Waddell, Esq., **191**
Sunnyside, **170**

Sunnyside, Tarrytown, New York, 4, **3, 170, 186**

Talcott Mountain, Hartford, Connecticut, 4
Tarrytown, New York, 5, **46**. SEE ALSO Lyndhurst, Tarrytown, New York
Ten Eyck, Henry, 6
Tennyson, Alfred, Lord, **114, 146**
Tichenor Isaac, **156**
Timmes, John, **59**
Timmes (or Timms), Peter, **59**
Tioranda, Dutchess County, New York, **36, 74**
Tom Tower, Christ Church, Oxford, 10
Town, Ithiel, 4
Trinity Church, New York, 3
Troy, New York, **30, 99, 157**
Tucker, William Ellis, Factory (ca. 1826–1838), **140**
Tuckermann, Henry, **180**

Underwood, William, **136**
Underwood, William, and Company, **136, 137**
Union College, Schenectady, New York, **155**
United States Pottery Company (1853–1858), **141**
Upjohn, Richard, 4, 6, **42, 67**

van Rensselaer, William P., **168**
van Ruisdael, Jacob, 3
Vanbrugh, Sir John, 2, 10
Vantilburg, Thomas L., **38**

Vassall-Longfellow House, Cambridge, Massachusetts, **89**
Virginia, **159**
Vose and Company (ca. 1848–1861), **158**

Waddell, William C., 7, **191**
Waddell House, **185, 191, 193**
Wadsworth, Daniel, 4
Walnut Wood, Bridgeport, Connecticut, 7, 8, **185, 191**
Walpole, Horace, 2, 8
Walter, Thomas Ustick (1804–1887), 8, **183**
Ward, The Four Children of Marcus L., **174**
Warner, Andrew Ellicott (1786–1870), **144**
Watson, John F., **118**
"Wedding Cake House," Kennebunk, Maine, 6
Wells, Joseph C., 6, **21, 187, 192**
Wheeler, Nathaniel, **185**
White House, Washington, D.C., **3, 4, 176**
White Plains, New York, **12, 15, 60, 70**
Whitmore, Gilbert D. (active 1843–1865), **18**
Whittredge, Thomas Worthington (1820–1910), **171 and n**
Willis, Nathaniel P., 1
Winslow, James, 6
Wren, Sir Christopher, 2, 10
Wyatt, James, 2

Designed by Robert C. Lewis. Text composed in English Monotype Plantin with title display in Engravers Old English. Printed on Warren's Cameo Dull Coated at the Press of A. Colish in Mount Vernon, New York. Binding by Publishers Book Bindery, Long Island City, New York.

First Printing, 1976: 2500 copies